Talkback
Trash and Treasure

Wit, Wisdom and Wireless

Stephanie Marsden

R&R Publications Marketing

For my Mum,
who taught me how to listen.

Published by:
R&R Publications Marketing Pty Ltd
ACN 083 612 579
PO Box 254 Carlton North, Victoria 3054
National Toll-free: 1 800 063 296
Publisher: Richard Carroll
Author: Stephanie Marsden
Cover Design: Carlton Studios
Layout and Design: Jenny Ring
Editing and Proofreading: Jenny Ring

The National Library of Australia
Cataloguing-in-Publication Data

Marsden, Stephanie
  Talkback Trash & Treasure
  ISBN 1 875655 91 3
  1. Radio Stories—Australia 2. Talk shows—Australia
  I. Title. II. Title: Talkback Trash & Treasure
791.4460994

First printed July 1999
Printed by Tat Wei Printing Packaging Pte Ltd, Singapore
Computer typeset in Galliard, Kabel, Freestyle Script, Boulevard,
  American Typewriter, Caslon Antique, Aachen, Brush Script,
  Monotype Pepita, Eras and Rosewood.

Ah, it makes me smile and it makes me glad,
It makes me laugh and it makes me sad,
From the day I was born to the day I go,
I want to listen to the radio.
Yeah, it lifts me up and it turns me on,
It stays by my side till the night is gone,
From the day I was born till the day I go
I want to listen to the radio.

Jingle heard daily on
5DN's Jeremy Cordeaux Show
(P. Best, 1980 CBS Records Australia)

To all Members of our Talkback Family:

You may be surprised to learn that in any face-to-face communication between humans, only 7 percent of our message is transmitted in the actual words we speak. 93 percent of what we're telling someone is non-verbal. Our body language makes up 55 percent and the tone of the voice conveys 38 percent.

So your favourite radio talkshow host is operating, at best, on a mere 45 percent communication capacity—you too, whenever you share your views over the talkback line. And unless you've met, each of you has only a hazy mental image of the other while you're speaking.

Producers are aware that, for many callers, the effort of getting on air can be both time-consuming and nerve-wracking. Your courage and endurance are greatly appreciated. Despite the inevitable hot ear and stiff arm, stay tuned and don't stop dialling. It's thanks to you that thousands of listeners now know . . .

- that the most comfortable mattress in any motel room is the one furthest from the phone,

- that your neutered pet can now have prosthetic nuticles fitted and they come in five sizes,

- that more information has been published in the last thirty years than in the past five thousand,

- and that people who load their toilet roll holders with the sheets over rather than under are 80 percent more likely to be lolly crunchers than lolly suckers?

Stephanie Marsden

Contents

Clockwise from top left: Terry Laidler (3LO); Alan Jones (2UE); Richard Glover (2BL);
Andrew Harwood (2UE); Howard Sattler(6PR); Jeremy Cordeaux (5DN) and John Vincent.

A Tribute to Talkback

From Valves to Vietnam

Although radio as entertainment was introduced to Australia in the early 1920s, the Golden Age of Radio captivated the nation in the 1940s and '50s. So great was its impact, it moved the focus of most families from the traditional hearth to a handsome box of glowing valves.

In those simpler, more subdued days radio was the medium of the imagination and excitement, the ultimate escape. Through it people could take control of their aural diet. There were live quiz shows, children's clubs, amateur hours, and the original soap operas.

Personalities such as Jack Davey, Queenie Ashton and Bob Dyer became stars of the sitting room. Serials titled *Blue Hills*, *When A Girl Marries*, *Portia Faces Life* and *Doctor Paul* were so locked into listeners' daily lives, small children were convinced a cast of tiny people lived in the back of the box.

Then came television, and with it brash reality in all its graphic glory. And in less than a decade a fresh young nation, bloodied but unsullied by a depression and two world wars, finally lost its innocence. Forgotten in sheds and attics around the country, those handsome old valve radios now gathered dust.

Dial-in Democracy

From the moment that 2GB's John Pearce first opened up the talkback lines in Australia in April 1967, politicians nationwide must have felt uncomfortably exposed and accountable. While teams of media advisers were hired to deal with the hazards at their end of the telephone, the voting public at the other end started taking a closer interest in what was being said, done and changed on their behalf.

Suddenly, to the isolated and housebound, human contact was only as far away as their trannie. They could now become involved, articulate their views, air their problems, offer solutions. *They could make a difference*. And all for the cost of a local phone call.

The Power of Talk Radio

For immediate and widespread distribution of information, no other medium compares or competes with talk radio—not television, not newspapers, not even the Internet. It's as accessible and portable as the digit that adjusts the dial.

Talk radio treads the shortest track to the senses. In an instant it can ignite anger and soothe the spirit. It has the power to alert, amuse, befriend, educate, prepare and inspire. Talk radio has made the world more aware; of injustice and inequality, of the helpless and the heroes, the comedies and conspiracies. Aware, too, of the price we must pay for freedom, good health and happiness.

To Whom It May Concern

It's thanks to the generosity of talkback listeners who were moved to make the call or send the fax (many of which, incidentally, were rescued from studio waste bins) that this book became a reality. While recording the best and worst of those contributions in *Talkback Trash & Treasure: Wit, Wisdom & Wireless*, an effort has been made to find and acknowledge the authors. But most of the truly memorable items have long since mislaid their origins in the mists of time, repetition and familiarity.

Talkback Man

He's rescuing a maiden from a dragon gross and green,
Or raising funds to purchase a dialysis machine.
He dominates the airwaves and his heart is Phar Lap size,
The families on struggle street all praise him to the skies.
The listeners love his music and even like his jokes,
He's the favourite of the sheilas and a leader for the blokes.

He's encouraging young athletes who'll be our future
    stars,
And helping nail the criminals who deal in stolen cars.
He's fighting for the widows and the veterans of our wars,
We know him as the champion of every worthy cause.
For victims of bureaucracy he's hope and inspiration.
His interviews are keenly sought by leaders of the nation.

The world's best entertainers have all been on his show.
He's asking each Australian to get up and have a go.
He respects each honest battler who's trying to make
    a quid.
If there's a dark and murky brew our man will lift the lid.
So if you face disaster, or just want to have a moan,
Tune in to radio's finest and pick up your telephone.

Australian performance bush poet
Michael Darby

Who Does What in a Commercial Talk Radio Station

General Manager: Responsible for the overall management.

Station Manager: Runs the budgeting, billing, reports, staff and services.

Technical Manager: Takes care of the technical staff, operating procedures, installation and repair of systems.

Sales Manager: Looks after the station's source of revenue, co-ordinates sales staff and agency reps.

Administration: Often covers such departments as Schedules (where and when the commercials are played), Accounting, Secretarial and Reception.

Program Director: Responsible for presenters, producers, content of programs and forward planning.

Promotions: In charge of all on and off air promotional activities, competitions and prizes.

Creative: The brains who not only create the commercials, but supervise the recording.

Production: The technical genius who times, helps put together and records all program segments and commercials.

Traffic: Makes sure all these segments, commercials and any regular features from external sources are aired on the right day at the right time.

Marketing: Thinks up new ways to make money for the station and helps advertising clients brainstorm ideas.

Talkback Tips and Tricks

All it takes to become a talkback star is practice and preparation. As you may have discovered, airing your views over the radio can become quite addictive. It's the strangest thing. You probably would be paralysed with fear at the prospect of public speaking, but may not think twice about lifting a receiver and sharing your most intimate secrets with tens of thousands of listeners.

Admittedly there's an element of anonymity; many callers adopt a nom-de-phone. And speaking from the comfort of your own home offers some reassurance.

Despite this you should be aware that a huge audience will be hanging on your every word, that your thoughts will be recorded both onto a master tape in the studio and a cassette tape in the production booth, that media monitoring organisations and politicians will take a close professional interest in your opinions, and that the presenter is likely to challenge your message.

After all, it is the task of a commercial radio show host to turn all words that flow up and down the airwaves into entertainment—entertainment that translates into healthy radio ratings. Popularity pays the bills.

Getting Through

Be organised. Even if you have only seconds to think about the point you wish to make, write it down before dialling the talkback number. And use your first words over the air to express that point firmly and clearly. You can qualify or argue your opinion immediately afterwards. Try to avoid repeating yourself.

Watch the clock. Don't launch into a new subject or major issue four minutes before a half-hourly news /update or hourly news broadcast. You might think there's enough time to say your piece, but the presenter may have to slot in a two-minute commercial commitment before the pips.

Take note of the program structure. Between dawn and the end of drive-time your favourite talkshow probably sticks fairly closely to a running sheet (see sample below). This is a tightly timed menu of interviews, pre-recordings, promotional items, advertisements and live studio featured guests, with space allowed for caller comment.

Overnight things loosen up considerably, so there's more time for talkback contributions. In fact, some night-time and, of course, lifestyle programs rely almost entirely on callers for their content.

Develop a talent for talkback. Producers always welcome articulate callers who help to open up a subject, even if they disagree with the presenter.

Dos and Don'ts

Don't drink and dial, unless you're absolutely sure you're not tiresome when you've tied one on. Your tape recorder will reveal the horrible truth. And hold off on the mind-altering medication until after you've made the call.

Do make notes before contacting the station's talk line. Good talkback demands a clear head and gathered thoughts.

Don't leave the phone once you've been placed in the switchboard queue. Waiting for your turn by listening to the radio doesn't work. There's a seven-second delay.

Do turn off your radio as soon as you get through. You'll hear the show down the phone line.
Helpful hint: if the line is constantly engaged, stay tuned to your radio, check the clock to make sure there's time for more calls, then press redial as soon as you believe the caller on air is just about to finish. Keep pressing redial until you hear the ringing tone.

Don't be offended if, having been kept waiting for ten or more minutes, the host goes to an interview or plays a batch of commercials. These are logged into the schedule and the studio computer so he/she may not have a choice. The producer will ask if you mind hanging on a bit longer.

Don't use unacceptable language or try to tell jokes you wouldn't like your mum to hear. You are likely to be dumped for the seven second delay or cut off entirely.

Don't mention names if you have a complaint against a person or organisation unless invited to do so.

Don't waste the presenter's or your time asking for a record request to be played during a show that is mostly newstalk or talkback.

Don't be tempted to read a prepared speech over the air. Lacking spontaneity it could sound contrived.

And finally:

Do feel free to share with listeners any brief amusing or moving verse and words of wit and wisdom. But please be prepared to provide the program's producer with a copy.

Running Sheet: Wednesday 25th June

{fictional sample only}

National Young Image Day

9.15 **Sybil Emery:** (Perth) *Mother of Clair, a 13-year-old anorexic.* Blames teen magazines like Go Girl for encouraging young girls to follow waif-like role models.

Lydia Grant: (Sydney) *Editor of Go Girl magazine.* Insists her publication is promoting a healthy image.

9.30 **Newsbreak/Finance Report**

9.40 **Cindy Cobbley:** (Alice Springs) *Field Officer, Fauna Protection Society.* Warns stricter regulations are needed if native animals are to be harvested for export. (Tasmanian possums already a delicacy in Asia)

10.00 **News/Sports Report**

10.10 **Keith Garelly:** *Emergency Services spokesman.* Says it's the responsibility of all people living in flood-prone regions of Australia to make sure they have flood insurance cover, and not rely on state aid.

10.20 **Anne Fosdike:** (studio) *Business consultant.* Setting up local enterprise agency for school leavers.

10.30 **News Update/Technology Report**

10.35 **Joe Dunn:** *City councillor.* Concerned at the cost of making our parks and malls more people-friendly.

10.50 **Ray Carter**: (Hollywood) *PAN gossip columnist* with latest showbiz news.

11.00 News/Sports Report

11.10 Wal Jonstone: (Ellinore, NT) *Farmer* building a biosphere and theme park on his outback property.

11.20 Dr Shah Patel: (Melbourne) *Oncologist and Director of the Holder Cancer Research Unit.* Hitting the headlines worldwide with a breast cancer breakthrough.

11.30 News Update/Afternoon Program Promos

11.35 Mid-week Soapbox

11.50 Brian Kernel: *21-year-old Gold Coast barman and bouncer* who entered a Charity Queen contest—and won.

12.00 News

How a Running Sheet Works

Although a newstalk producer tries to stick to the schedule, it's not always possible. People lined up for an interview may become suddenly unavailable at the time specified, or a studio guest may be stuck in traffic with a flat mobile phone battery.

Also a major breaking news event generally takes priority over everything. In that case the producer and production assistant, if any, will be flat out liaising closely with the newsroom, finding someone to comment on or describe the event and keeping the program's host supplied with broadcastable information.

In the confusion talkback callers may feel sorely neglected. This is unfortunate but often unavoidable. Many major talk radio stations are now fully computerised and supposedly nearing paper-free-zone status. But not all.

So the presenter and producer will each have a printout of the Running Sheet, and a copy is handed to the newsroom journalists to tell them when someone newsworthy will be on air, and to the receptionist who may need to answer listener enquiries.

Yet another copy is placed in the Production Booth Logbook where it stays for at least a week. This enables overnight presenters and producers of later shows to check on interviews and issues already covered and, again, allows them to pass on information to you, the listeners, without whom the program—indeed, the radio station itself—would be pointless.

The Human Condition

Mark Twain said it and talkback confirms it, 'Man is the only animal that blushes—or needs to'. At least no-one notices over the radio. Wouldn't it be so much easier to play our part in life if we had a copy of the script?

Thanks to tireless researchers, some of the bigger questions we face each day have been answered; for instance, why does a bride wear white? Because it's the colour of all kitchen appliances. But a listener survey revealed there are still a few we'd like them to work on.

20 Mysteries of the Universe

1 Why do soldiers patrolling in cities wear jungle camouflage?

2 Why is it, when the doorbell rings, the dog always thinks it's for him?

3 How does Teflon stick to the pan?

4 How come slow down means the same as slow up?

5 How does Dracula shave if he can't see his reflection in the mirror?

6 If I said I always tell lies, would I be telling the truth?

7 Why are people in the Second World never mentioned?

8 If moths are attracted to light, why don't they come out during the day?

9 How do we know God likes hymns?

10 Where did the man who invented patents register his idea?

11 What is the speed of dark?

12 Why do slugs never eat weeds?

13 Why don't people who believe in reincarnation leave their money to themselves?

14 What do occasional tables do for the rest of the time?

15 How come airline meal trays are fuller after you've finished eating?

16 Why are vices more habit-forming than virtues?

17 Where do people in hell tell each other to go?

18 Why do they bother to sterilise the needle when giving a lethal injection?

19 Why is a wrong number never engaged?

20 And why do kamikaze pilots wear crash helmets?

Why can't Life's big problems come when we are twenty, and know everything?

Life rarely lightens up on its supply of stumbling blocks, the largest being the fact that there are always more victors than spoils. To get an edge, try these . . .

Give-It-a-Go Guidelines

Life rarely lightens up on its supply of stumbling blocks, the largest being the fact that there are always more victors than spoils. To get an edge, try these . . .

- Beware; the toes you tread on today may belong to the feet that are attached to the legs that hold up the arse you may have to kiss tomorrow.

- Live every day as if it's your last. One day you'll be right.

- Only an average person is always at his/her best.

- People who matter don't mind. People who mind, don't matter.

- The reason it's so difficult to make ends meet is, someone is always moving the ends.

- 'I must do something' will always solve more problems than 'something must be done'.

- If at first you don't succeed—cheat.

- It's easier to get forgiveness than permission.

- Inside every small problem is a major disaster trying to get out.

- If something is worth doing, it's worth telling someone how to do it well.

- When faced with two evils, always pick the one you haven't tried before.

- People will believe anything if you whisper it.

Why Company Vehicles are So Popular

A recent report lists some superior features not found in private cars.

- A company car travels faster in all gears, especially reverse.
- They accelerate at a phenomenal rate.
- They need a much shorter braking distance.
- They have a much tighter turning circle.
- They can take ramps at twice the speed of a private vehicle.
- Battery, oil, water and tyre pressures don't need to be checked nearly as often.
- They don't need to be garaged at night.
- They can be driven an extra 200 km with the oil warning light flashing.
- They require cleaning, especially inside, less often.
- Tyre walls are designed for bumping safely into and over high kerbs.
- They are adapted to allow reverse gear to be engaged while the car is still moving forward.
- They have reinforced suspension permitting the transportation of concrete and other heavy building materials.
- The floor is shaped like an ashtray.
- Unusual and alarming engine noises are easily eliminated by adjusting the radio volume control.
- No security is necessary. They can be left anywhere, unlocked, with the keys in the ignition.

The loudest noise in the world is the first rattle in your new car.

And in case you hadn't noticed: Life is what happens to us while we're making other plans. In spite of the cost of living, it's still surprisingly popular.

Next time you press the 'up' button in a crowded lift, raise the spirits of other elevatees with these rib-ticklers, guaranteed to put the chuck into chuckle:

Give 'em a Lift and a Laugh

- Open your handbag or briefcase a couple of centimetres, look in, and ask, 'Got enough air in there?'
- Grimace painfully, put your hand to your forehead and say, 'Shut up, damn it! All of you, just *shut up!*'
- Stare and grin at another passenger and announce, 'I've got new socks on'.
- Bet the other passengers you can fit a ten cent piece up your nose.
- Answer your mobile phone, look outraged and shout, 'What the hell do you mean I should plead criminally insane!'
- Turn to face elevatees, look serious and state, 'I suppose you're wondering why I've called you to this meeting'.

You don't want to know this, but Christmas is the most hazardous time for family relationships, and January is the top month for marriage break-ups. They should call it the Stresstival Season.

The Four Stages of Man

When you believe in Santa Claus
When you don't believe in Santa Claus
When you are Santa Claus
When you look like Santa Claus

Life: no matter how thin you slice it, you're always left with two sides.

Whenever someone insists it's not the money, but it's the principle of the thing—it's the money.

Expressions like 'no man is an island' and 'for whom the bell tolls' are irresistible to a broadcaster. Their use implies an unlikely familiarity with the classics.

No Man is an Island

No man is an island, entire of itself; every man is a piece of the continent, a part of the main. If a clod be washed away by the sea, Europe is the less, as well as if a promontory were, as well as if a manor of thy friend's or of thine own were. Any man's death diminishes me because I am involved in mankind, and therefore never send to know for whom the bell tolls; it tolls for thee.

17th century poet John Donne

And for those of you who kept meaning to ask for them, here are those . . .

Ten Modern Laws

- People who eat natural food die of natural causes.
- A politician will always be there when he needs you.
- If everyone else has a flu vaccination, you don't need one.
- If it wasn't for the last minute nothing would get done.
- Beware of buying anything where the manual is bigger than the equipment.
- You never want the one you can afford.
- Never play cat and mouse games if you're a mouse.
- Inflation allows you to live in a more expensive neighbourhood without moving.
- Your favourite song always comes on the car radio when you reach your destination.
- Good judgement comes from experience, and experience comes from bad judgement.

The Affluence of Incohol

I had twelve bottles of whisky in my cellar, and was told by my wife to empty the contents of each and every bottle down the sink—or else. So I said I would, then proceeded with the unpleasant task.

I withdrew the cork from the first bottle and poured the liquor down the sink, with the exception of one glass, which I drank. I pulled the cork from the second bottle and did likewise, with the exception of one glass, which I drank.

I withdrew the cork from the third bottle and poured the whisky down the sink, which I drank. I pulled the bottle from the cork of the next and drank one sink of it, and the rest down the glass.

I pulled the sink out of the next glass, and poured the cork down the bottle. Then I corked the sink with the glass, bottled the drink and drank the pour.

When I had everything emptied, I steadied the house with one hand and counted the glasses, corks, bottles and sinks with the other, which were twenty-nine; and as the house came by, I counted them again, and finally had all the house in one bottle which I drank.

I am not under the affluence of incohol, but some thinkle peep I am—I am not half to thunk as you may drink. I fool so feelish, and don't know who is me, and the drunker I stand here the longer I get . . . hic.

A Toast

My love to all those who I love,
My love to all those who love me.
My love to all those who love those who I love,
And to those who love those who love me.

When we surrendered our old dial phones, little did we know we'd be placing ourselves at the mercy of answering machines, hold music and sinister recorded voices— voices that refuse us access to a human until we've passed a tricky Touchphone IQ Test.

Pushing the Right Buttons

Welcome to the Psychiatrists' Telephone Hotline. Please hold on and follow these instructions:

- If you are obsessive compulsive, press 1 repeatedly.

- If you have multiple personalities, press 2, 3 and 4.

- For advice on paranoia, we know who you are and what you really want—stay on the line so we can trace your call.

- If your problem is schizophrenia, listen carefully and a little voice will tell you which number to press.

- And if you are delusional, press hash immediately and stand away from the receiver before it bites your ear.

The secret of success in all things is, of course . . .

Don't Quit

When things go wrong as they sometimes will,
When the road you're trudging seems all uphill,
When the funds are low and the debts are high,
And you want to smile, but you have to sigh,
When care is pushing you down a bit
Rest if you must—but don't quit.

Success is failure turned inside out,
The silver tint on the clouds of doubt.
And you never can tell how close you are,
It may be near when it seems afar.
So stick to the fight when you're hardest hit.
It's when things go wrong that you must not quit.

Only a few years ago members of the thought police insisted that all expressions where black was used in a negative context—black mark, accident black spot, black Friday—were racially offensive. 'Ban them', they cried. Which persuaded a caller to share with us . . .

Who're You Calling Coloured?

Dear white fella,

A couple of things you oughta know.
Firstly . . .

When I was born, I was black.
When I grew up, I was black.
When I choke, I'm black.
When I'm scared, I'm black.
When I get sick, I'm black.
When I go out in the sun, I'm black.
When I get cold, I'm black
And when I die, I'm still black.

But you, white fella . . .
When you were born, you were pink.
When you grew up, you were white.
When you choke, you're blue.
When you're scared, you're yellow.
When you get sick, you're green.
When you go out in the sun, you're red.
When you get cold, you're blue.
And when you die, you go purple.

**And you've got the cheek
to call me coloured!**

And on the subject of cheek . . .
Justice is the system by which every man gets what's coming to him.
Law is the system by which you make damn sure he doesn't.

2 Battle of the Sexes

New York's famous feminists, the Guerilla Girls, blame the male of the species for most domestic and global aggression. Their solution for bringing peace to the world is awe-inspiring. They want to create an Oestrogen Bomb. When it's dropped on an area of violent conflict, men will 'throw down their guns, hug each other, apologise, say it was "all their fault" and then start to clean up the mess'. The trouble with conflict is it's more likely to determine who is left, than who is right . . .

Ten Things Women Do That Irritate Men

- Stuff the car ashtray with Kleenex
- Keep your embarrassing love letters
- Point out the streaks on the glasses you've washed up
- Try to make you eat healthier food
- Read magazine articles which suggest your libido is seriously below average
- Treat plants like children
- Want to get engaged
- Say 'Don't you think you've had enough to drink?'
- Drag you to the sales
- Wonder why you need to go to the pub when there's plenty of beer in the fridge.

Ten Things Men Do That Irritate Women

- Leave the toilet seat up
- Suggest that a woman at home all day has nothing to do
- Leave dirty socks inside out
- Claim total inability to work the washing machine
- Forget to cut their toenails
- Throw wet towels on the bed
- Compliment other women on their clothes
- Leave used sports gear in a bag or car boot for weeks
- Buy presents of utterly impractical underwear
- Feel insecure if a woman earns more than they do

quoted from the *UK Mail on Sunday,* *YOU* **magazine**

Nice Men Never

Nice men never lie to you,
Nice men never flatter;
Nice men never madden you,
Nice men never matter.

English poet John Turnbull

Q: Why are girls so biased?

A: It's always bias this and bias that . . .

You can soon tell who's boss in the family, it's the one who takes charge of the TV remote control. But as far as this catalogue of comparisons is concerned, it's still a man's world.

Why Women Can Never Win

A businessman is dynamic.
A businesswoman is aggressive.

A businessman is good on details.
She is . . . picky.

He is assertive.
She is bitchy.

He's a go-getter.
She's pushy.

When he's depressed he's been working too hard.
When she's moody, it must be her time of the month.

He follows through.
She doesn't know when to quit.

He's confident.
She's stuck up.

He stands firm.
She's hard as nails.

He has the courage of his convictions.
She's plain stubborn.

He's a man of the world.
She's been around.

He can handle his liquor.
She's a lush.

He isn't afraid to say what he thinks.
She's a big mouth.

He's a warm human being.
She's emotional.

He exercises authority diligently.
She is power mad.

He is discreet.
She's secretive.

He can make quick decisions.
She's impulsive.

He's a stern taskmaster.
She's hard to work for.

He climbed the ladder of success.
She Slept Her Way to the Top!

> There are only two kinds of women—goddesses and doormats.
>
> *Picasso*

> A woman is like a teabag. You can't tell how strong she is until you put her in hot water.
>
> *Nancy Reagan*

Until recently, males at the mike with shock-jock aspirations labelled women's libbers 'Feminazis, The Hairy Armpit Brigade and Pinko-Lesbo Bra-Burning Ball-Busters'. It's no wonder the fair sex fought back with . . .

A Salvo from the Sisterhood

Because a woman's work is never done and is underpaid or unpaid or boring or repetitious and we're the first to get the sack and what we look like is more important than what we do and if we get raped it's our own fault and if we get bashed we must have provoked it and if we raise our voices we're nagging bitches and if we enjoy sex we're nymphos and if we don't we're frigid and if we love women it's because we can't get a 'real' man and if we ask our doctor too many questions we're neurotic and/or pushy and if we expect community care for children we're selfish

25

and if we stand up for our rights we're aggressive and unfeminine and if we don't we're typical weak females and if we want to get married we're out to trap a man and if we don't we're unnatural and because we still can't get an adequate safe contraceptive but men can walk on the moon and if we can't cope with or don't want a pregnancy we're made to feel guilty about abortion and . . . for lots and lots of other reasons we are part of the women's liberation movement.

No worries. All it takes to counter that artillery of female angst is . . .

A Blast from the Brothers

- If you put a woman on a pedestal and try to protect her from the rat race, you're a male chauvinist pig. If you stay home and do the housework, you're a pansy.
- If you work too hard to bring home the bacon, you never have enough time for the missus and kids. If you don't work hard enough, you're a good-for-nothing layabout.
- If she has a boring repetitive job with low pay, that's exploitation. If you have a boring, repetitive job with low pay, you should get off your butt and find something better.
- If a man gets promotion ahead of a woman, that's favouritism. If she gets promotion ahead of him, that's equal opportunity.
- If he mentions how nice she looks, that's sexual harassment. If he doesn't, that's typical male indifference.
- If he cries, he's a sheila. If he doesn't, he's insensitive.
- If her man thumps her, that's wife bashing. If she thumps him, that's self defence.
- If he makes a decision without consulting her, that's male domination. If she makes a decision without regard to his feelings, she's a liberated woman.
- If he asks her to do something she doesn't enjoy, he's high-handed and bossy. If she asks him, it's a favour.
- If he appreciates the female form in frilly underwear, he's a sexual pervert. If he doesn't, he's a poofter.
- If he likes a woman to keep in shape and shave her legs, that's sexist. If he doesn't care, he's unromantic.

- If he tries to keep himself in shape, that's vanity. If he doesn't, he's a slob.
- If he buys her flowers, he's feeling guilty or is after something. If he doesn't, he's thoughtless and neglectful.
- If he's proud of his achievements, he's up himself. If he isn't, he lacks ambition.
- If she has a headache, it's because she's tired. If he has a headache, it's because he doesn't love her any more.
- If he wants it too often, he's oversexed. If he can't perform on cue, there must be somebody else.

**No wonder men are
bloody confused!**

You may recognise the next six items. In one form or another they've been turning up on office and studio fax machines throughout the English-speaking world for years. The 'cucumber' list has been censored somewhat for family consumption.

Why It's Great to Be a Guy

- Phone conversations are over in 30 seconds flat.
- Your underwear is $10 for a three-pack.
- A beer gut does not make you invisible to the opposite sex.
- You don't have to shave below your neck.
- Three pairs of shoes are more than enough.
- The remote control is yours and yours alone.
- People never stare at your chest when you're talking to them.

Why It's Great to Be a Girl

- We can wear pants *and* skirts.
- We can own 20 pairs of shoes.
- We can show our feelings and not be seen as sissy.
- We don't have to shave every day.
- We can exploit male pride to get yukky jobs done.
- If all else fails, we can burst into tears.
- Best of all, we got off the Titanic first.

Why a Beer Is Better than a Woman

- There's no 'time of the month' for a beer.
- You don't have to wine and dine a beer.
- There's no such thing as 'beer's prerogative' as an excuse for being late.
- Beer never has a headache.
- Beer is always wet.
- Your beer will wait patiently in the car while you fish.
- You can share a beer with friends.
- A beer doesn't get jealous when you grab another beer.
- A frigid beer is a good beer.
- A beer doesn't care when you come home.
- When you change beers you don't have to pay maintenance.

Why a Cucumber Is Better than a Man

- Most cucumbers are more than 20 centimetres long.
- Cucumbers are easy to pick up.
- You can fondle a cucumber in a supermarket.
- Cucumbers aren't jealous of your hairdresser or gynaecologist.
- A cucumber will always respect you in the morning.
- With a cucumber, you never have to say you're sorry.
- A cucumber will never make a scene because you have other cucumbers in the fridge.
- Cucumbers don't give you stubble rash or drool on the pillow.
- Cucumbers never leave the toilet seat up.
- No matter how old you are, you can always get hold of a fresh cucumber.
- You don't have to wait until half-time to talk to your cucumber.
- You always know where your cucumber has been.
- It's easy to dump a cucumber.
- You won't find out later your cucumber is married, infected or having it off with your best friend.

Hazardous Materials Report

Element: Woman

Mass (always critical): Varies from 45 kg to 245 kg

Active location: Large deposits in urban areas, scattered rural deposits.

Physical Properties:
- Surface normally obscured by paint.
- Boils at zero degrees and freezes spontaneously.
- Melts when alcohol is applied.
- Found in various grades from virgin to common ore.

Chemical Properties:
- Affinity to gold, silver, platinum and precious gems.
- Readily absorbs expensive substances.
- Explosive under lunar influence.
- Softens and takes on rosy glow in hot, soapy water.
- Turns red when discovered in the natural state.
- Turns green when placed alongside a superior specimen.

Common Uses:
- Is highly ornamental and an effective aid to relaxation.

The Rules

1 The female always makes **The Rules**.
2 **The Rules** are subject to change at any time without prior notification.
3 No male can possibly know all **The Rules**.
4 If the female suspects the male knows **The Rules**, she must immediately change some of or all **The Rules**.
5 The female is never wrong.
6 If the female is wrong it is because of a misunderstanding which was the direct result of something the male wrongly did or said.
7 If **Rule 6** applies, the male must apologise immediately for causing the misunderstanding.
8 The female can change her mind at any time.
9 The male must never change his mind without the express written consent of the female.
10 The female has the right to be upset or angry at any time.

11 The male must remain calm at all times unless the female wishes him to be angry or upset.

12 In no circumstances will the female give any indication to the male whether or not she wants him to be angry or upset.

13 Any attempt by the male to document **The Rules** may result in bodily harm.

14 If the female has PMS, all **The Rules** are null and void.

'I would hope that by the end of the 1990s there will be as many incompetent women running companies as men. Then we will be truly equal.'

Ita Buttrose

Marriage is the only adventure open to the cowardly.

This probably dates from the 1940s:

Men Are What Women Marry

They have two hands, two feet, sometimes two wives, but never more than one dollar or one idea at a time. Like Turkish cigarettes they are all made of the same material, the only difference being that some are more distinguished than others. Generally speaking they are divided into three categories, namely:

Bachelors, Widowers and Husbands

A bachelor is an eligible mass of obstinacy surrounded by suspicion.

A widower is a remnant with possibilities.

Husbands come in three types—prizes, surprises and consolation prizes.

Making a husband out of a man is one of the highest forms of plastic art known to civilisation. It requires science, sculpture, common sense, faith, hope and charity.

It is a psychological marvel that a small, tender, soft, violet-scented thing like a woman should want to kiss a big, awkward, stubble-chinned, tobacco-scented thing like a man.

If you flatter a man, you frighten him to death; if you don't, you bore him to death.

If you permit him to make love to you, he gets tired of you in the end; if you don't, he gets tired of you in the beginning.

If you wear gay colours, rouge and startling hats, he hesitates to take you out. If you wear a little brown hat and a tailored suit, he takes you out and stares at the other women in gay colours, rouge and startling hats.

If you join him in his gaieties and approve of his drinking, he swears you are leading him to the devil. If you don't approve of his drinking and urge him to give up his gaieties, he swears you are driving him to the devil.

If you are the clinging-vine type, he doubts that you have a brain. If you are the modern, independent type, he doubts that you have a heart.

If you are silly, he longs for an intelligent female. If you are intelligent, he is soon diverted by a frivolous female. If you are popular with men he is jealous. If you are not he hesitates to marry a wallflower.

A man is just a worm; he comes along, wriggles around for a while, and finally some bird gets him.

This Yuletide verse, harvested during some late night listening, is just too cute to cover up with the figleaf of censorship.

Der Liddle Fur Cap

Der next day vas Christmas, der night it vas schtill,
Der schtockings ver hung by der chimney to fill,
Der children ver dired und had gone to bet,
Und mudder in nightgoun, and I, going ahead,

Vas searching around in der closet for toys,
Ve crept around kviet not to raise any noise.
Now mudder vas carrying all her toys in her goun
Showing her person from der vaist down.

Ven, as ve came near der crib of our boy,
Our youngest and sveetest, our pride and our choy,
He opened vide his eyes as he peered from his cot
Und seed everything vot his mudder has got.

But he didn't notice der toys in her lap,
He chust asked, 'For who is dot liddle fur cap?'
Und mudder said, 'Hush', and laughed vid delight.
'I tink I give dot to your fadder tonight.'

Where would overnight talkback be without . . .

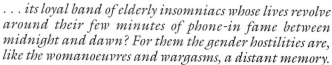

. . . *its loyal band of elderly insomniacs whose lives revolve around their few minutes of phone-in fame between midnight and dawn? For them the gender hostilities are, like the womanoeuvres and wargasms, a distant memory.*

But still they furnish the empty hours with warmth and wisdom, and some sonorous snoring if they spend too long on hold and the Mogadon kicks in. This little verse, dated 1907 and discovered in a listener's autograph book, is dedicated to them:

Truce

Sometimes when nothing goes just right,
And worries reign supreme,
When all the world looms dark as night
And all things useless seem,
There's just one thing can drive away
The tears that scald and blind.
Someone to slip a strong arm round
And whisper, 'Never mind'.

The Good Old Days

When you look back and see your past as The Good Old Days, that's when you realise you can't relive it; that memories are like corks left out of bottles—they swell and somehow don't fit any more. Your ambitions have long since been nipped in the budget, and you decide to be nice to your children because they'll soon be choosing your nursing home. And, somehow, nostalgia just isn't what it used to be . . .

For anyone aged under forty, these are the good old days the next generation will hear so much about. But . . .

How Do You Know When You're Getting Old?

- Everything hurts, and what doesn't hurt doesn't work.
- **The gleam in your eye is from the sun hitting your bifocals.**
- You feel like the 'morning after' but you haven't been anywhere the night before.
- **Your little black book contains only names starting with Dr.**
- You get winded playing chess.
- **Your children begin to look middle-aged.**
- You join a health club and don't go.
- **You decide to procrastinate but never get round to it.**
- A dripping tap causes an uncontrollable bladder urge.
- **You know all the answers, but nobody asks you the questions.**
- You look forward to a dull evening.
- **You walk with your head high—trying to get used to your new specs.**
- You turn out the lights for economic rather than romantic reasons.
- **You sit in a rocking chair and can't get it going.**
- Your knees buckle, but your belt won't.
- **You begin to regret all those times that you resisted temptation.**

- Dialling long distance wears you out.
- **You become intolerant of people who are intolerant.**
- The best part of your day is over when your alarm goes off.
- **You burn the midnight oil after 9pm.**
- Your back goes out more often than you do.
- **A fortune teller offers to read your face.**
- Your pacemaker makes the garage door go up when you watch a pretty girl pass by.
- **The little grey-haired old lady you help across the street is . . . your wife.**
- You get your exercise serving as a pallbearer at funerals of friends who exercised.
- **You have too much room in the house, but not enough in the medicine cabinet.**
- You sink your teeth into a steak, and they stay there.

Alzheimer's isn't so bad. Not only do you get to hide your own Easter Eggs, but you meet new people every day.

One blessing of old age is that you can stop trying to 'find yourself', because each day there are more urgent things to find—such as your specs and car keys.

Ode to Memory

Just a line to say I'm living,
I'm not among the dead,
Though I'm getting more forgetful
And mixed up in my head.

I've got used to my arthritis,
To my dentures I'm resigned.
I can handle my bifocals
But—oh God, I miss my mind!

Sometimes I can't remember
When I'm standing on the stair,
If I'm going up for something
Or I've just come down from there.

And before the fridge, so often,
My mind is filled with doubt.
Now, did I put some food away
Or come to take some out?

And sometimes during night-time,
With confusion in my head,
I don't know if I'm getting in
Or getting out of bed!

If it's not my turn to write, dear,
I hope you won't feel sore.
I may think that I have written
And do not want to bore.

So, remember, I think of you
And wish that you lived near.
And now it's time to mail this
And say 'goodbye' my dear.

Later:
I stand before the mailbox,
Again, confusion in my head.
I should have posted this to you
But I've opened it instead!

Yesterday is history, tomorrow is a mystery, today is a gift—that's why it's called the present; and there's no-one more aware of this than the person born before 1940 . . .

The Survivors

We were around before television, before penicillin, polio shots, frozen foods, Xerox, plastic, contact lenses, videos, frisbees and the pill.

We were born before radar, credit cards, split atoms, laser beams and ballpoint pens; before dishwashers, tumble dryers, electric blankets, air fresheners, drip-dry clothes . . . and before men walked on the moon.

We got married first, and then lived together.

We thought 'fast food' was what you ate in Lent, a 'big Mac' was an oversized raincoat and 'crumpet' was something we had for tea.

We existed before house-husbands, computer dating and dual careers, and when a 'meaningful relationship' meant getting along with cousins, and 'sheltered accommodation' was where you waited for a bus.

We were before day care centres, group homes and disposable nappies.

We never heard of FM radio, tape decks, laptop computers, genetic engineering, artificial hearts, mobile phones and young men wearing earrings.

For us 'time sharing' meant togetherness, a 'chip' was a piece of wood or fried potato, 'hardware' meant nuts and bolts and 'software' wasn't even a word.

The term 'making out' referred to how you did in your exams, 'stud' was something that fastened a collar to a shirt and 'going all the way' meant staying on the bus to the terminus.

Pizzas, McDonalds and instant coffee were unheard of.

In our day cigarette smoking was fashionable, 'grass' was mown, 'coke' was kept in the coal shed, a 'joint' was a piece of meat you had on Sundays and 'pot' was something you cooked in.

'Rock music' was grandmother's lullaby, 'El Dorado' was an ice cream and 'gay' simply meant lively and merry.

We who were born before 1940 must be a hardy bunch when you consider how the world has changed and the adjustments we've had to make. No wonder we're bewildered and there's a generation gap. But, by the Grace of God, we've survived!

Here are two of the most cherished pieces of verse in talkback territory. Sadly, the authors remain anonymous.

Crabbit Old Woman

What do you see, nurses, what do you see?
What are you thinking when you look at me?
A crabbit old woman, not very wise,
Uncertain of habit with faraway eyes,

Who dribbles her food and makes no reply,
When you say in a loud voice, 'I do wish you'd try'.
Who seems not to notice the things that you do,
And forever is losing a stocking or shoe.

Who, unresisting or not, lets you do as you will,
With bathing and feeding, the long day to fill.
Is that what you're thinking, is that what you see?
Then open your eyes. You're not looking at me!

I'll tell you who I am as I sit here so still,
As I move to your bidding, as I eat at your will.
I'm a small child of ten with a father and mother,
Brothers and sisters who love one another.

A young girl of sixteen with wings on her feet,
Dreaming that soon now a lover she'll meet.
A bride soon at twenty—my heart gives a leap
Remembering the vows that I promised to keep.

At twenty-five now I have young of my own
Who need me to build a secure, happy home.
A woman of thirty, children growing so fast,
Bound to each other with ties that should last.

At forty now, my young soon will be gone,
But my man stays beside me to see I don't mourn.
At fifty once more babies play round my knee,
Again we know children, my loved one and me.

Dark days are upon me, my husband is dead.
I look to the future, I shudder with dread.
My young are all busy, rearing babes of their own,
And I think of the years and the love I have known.

I'm an old woman now, and Nature is cruel,
'Tis her jest to make aged ones look like a fool.
The body it crumbles, grace and vigour depart,
And now there's a stone where I once had a heart.

But inside this old carcass a young girl still dwells,
And now and again my battered heart swells.

I remember the joy, the hopes and the pain
And I'm loving and living life over again.

I think of the years all too few—gone too fast,
And accept the stark fact that nothing can last.
So, open your eyes, nurses, open and see
Not a crabbit old woman. Look closer . . . see me.

The Nurse's Reply

What do we see? Oh, we have feelings, too.
And, yes, we are thinking when looking at you.
We may seem quite hard as we hurry and fuss,
But there's many of you and too few of us.

We would like far more time to sit by you and talk,
To bathe you and feed you and help you to walk;
To hear of your lives and the things you have done,
Your childhood, your husband, your daughter, your son.

But time is against us—there's too much to do,
Patients too many, and nurses too few.
We grieve when we see you so frail and alone,
With no-one to hear you, no friends of your own.

We feel all your pain, and know of your fear
That nobody cares now your end is so near.
But nurses are people with feelings as well,
And when we're together you'll often hear tell

Of the dearest old gran in the very end bed,
And the lovely old dad and the things that he said.
We speak with compassion, and also feel glad
As we think of the joys and adventures you've had.

When the time has arrived for you to depart,
You leave us behind with an ache in the heart.
When you sleep the long sleep—no more worry or care,
There are other old folk, and we must be there.

So please understand if we hurry and fuss.
There are many of you, and too few of us.

It's a sad reality of life that, by the time you reach those greener pastures of your dreams, you're too feeble to climb the fence.

Nothing promotes nostalgia so well as a good wine and a bad memory.

There was a time when you could rely on your mum to grow old gracefully, spending her 'declining' years baking goodies for the grandchildren and playing bowls or bingo. How things have changed . . .

Thoroughly Modern Granny

I have a little granny, she's really very old,

But very unconventional, in a most unusual mould.

She doesn't wear her spectacles perched upon her nose,

She's into contact lenses, and polishes her toes.

Unlike some other grannies who get home before it's dark,

She's dressed up in a track suit and jogging in the park.

And when I wish she'd sometimes stay and tuck me into bed,

She's off to study yoga, and standing on her head!

Some grannies sit in rocking chairs and knit and take their pills.

My granny's joined a hiking group and treks across the hills.

She goes on day trips with her gang, the over-60s club,

They rocket round the countryside and end up in the pub.

Then on the homeward journey like a flock of singing birds,

They harmonise old favourites, with very naughty words.

I love my little granny. I think she's really great,

If that's what growing old is like, I simply cannot wait!

The Happiest Years?

Which would you consider to be the age of greatest happiness? Childhood? Your twenties?

Actually it's **old age**.

A 1998 Fordham University survey confirms findings first reported by Gail Sheehy, author of *Pathfinders*. Both show that men generally are happiest in their middle sixties, and women during their seventies.

And the unhappiest time? That's the early fifties for men and late forties for women.

So who resists age best? **Creative people!**

The happiest people don't necessarily have the best of everything. But talkback tells us they do make the best of everything.

What Are Seniors Worth?

Dear friend, remember that us old folks are worth a fortune, with silver in our hair, gold in our teeth, stones in the kidneys, lead in our feet and gas in our stomachs.

While I may have become a little older since I saw you last, I have in the meantime become quite a frivolous old girl, having three gentlemen with me every day. Will Power helps me get out of bed each morning, and Arthur Ritis never leaves me alone. He doesn't like to stay in one place for long so we go from joint to joint.

After such a busy day I'm really tired and glad to go to bed with Johnny Walker. What a life! Oh yes, and I'm flirting with Al Zymer.

The preacher came to call the other day. He said at my age I should be thinking of the hereafter. I told him: 'Oh, I do that all the time. No matter where I am, in the living room, the kitchen or upstairs, I'm always asking myself—what am I here after?'

It's easy to work out which is your station in life. Sooner or later someone will tell you where to get off.

A definition of nostalgia: when you find the present tense, and the past perfect. Which brings us to that proudly patriotic perennial that crops up whenever challengers seek to change the flag.

Our Flag

Our flag bears the stars that blaze at night,
In our Southern sky of blue,
And that little old flag in the corner,
That's part of our heritage, too.
It's not for the English, the Scots and the Irish

Who were sent to the end of the earth,
The rogues and the schemers, the doers and dreamers
Who gave modern Australia its birth.

And you who are shouting to change it,
You don't seem to understand,
It's the flag of our laws and our language
Not the flag of a faraway land.
There are lots of people who'll tell you
How, when Europe was plunged into night,
That little old flag in the corner
Was their symbol of freedom and light.

It doesn't mean we owe our allegiance
To a forgotten imperial dream.
We've the stars to show where we're going,
And the old flag to show where we've been.
It's only an old piece of bunting,
It's only an old coloured rag,
But there are thousands who fought for its honour
And sacrificed all for our flag.

It's a dial-in debate that never fails to scorch the switchboard. Should our national anthem be changed?

Invariably I Still Call Australia Home *and* Song of Australia *are suggested alternatives. But whether young and free or getting on and mortgaged to the hilt, it's still a good idea to learn the words to your nation's number one song, even if 'girt by sea' does make you squirm. You never know when you might be called upon to pretend to sing it . . .*

The Australian National Anthem

Australians all let us rejoice,
For we are young and free;
We've golden soil and wealth for toil,
Our home is girt by sea.
Our land abounds in nature's gifts
Of beauty rich and rare;
In history's page, let every stage
Advance Australia Fair.
In joyful strains then let us sing,
Advance Australia Fair.

Beneath our radiant Southern Cross
We'll toil with hearts and hands,
To make this Commonwealth of ours
Renowned for all the lands.
For those who've come across the seas
We've boundless plains to share,
With courage let us all combine
To Advance Australia Fair.
In joyful strains then let us sing,
Advance Australia Fair.

Thirty-odd years ago . . .

. . . a record (45 rpm Allan's MX-25680) was released featuring the GTV Channel 9 orchestra and vocalist Neil Williams performing a stirring new anthem (Cowan-O'Hagan) to the tune of Waltzing Matilda. *Even in the late 1990s, whenever it was played on the air callers voted it a winner. Here are the not-quite-PC but still powerful words to . . .*

God Bless Australia

Here in this God-given land of ours, Australia,
This proud possession, our own piece of earth;
That was built by our fathers who pioneered our heritage
Here in Australia, the land of our birth.

Chorus
God bless Australia, our land Australia,
Home of the Anzac, the strong and the free,
It's our homeland, our own land,
To cherish for eternity.
God bless Australia, the land of the free.

Here in Australia we treasure love and liberty,
Our way of life, all for one, one for all.
We're a peace-loving race but should danger ever
    threaten us,
Let the world know we will answer the call.

Chorus
God bless Australia, our land Australia . . .

When saving for your old age, be sure to tuck away a few pleasant thoughts.

World War One veteran to well-meaning young man at the mike on Anzac Day: 'It's time you learnt to show some respect, sonny. Having reached the age of ninety-five, it makes me cranky when some patronising, wet-behind-the-ears whippersnapper tries to tell me over the wireless I'm ninety-five years **young**. You wouldn't call a priceless Ming vase 500 years young, would you?'

And to remind us of just how 'utopian' the good old days must have seemed to nineteenth century workers . . .

Merchants and Ships Chandlers
Sydney Town 1852

RULES FOR CLERICAL STAFF

1 Godliness, Cleanliness and Punctuality are the necessities of a good Business.

2 On the recommendation of the Governor of this Colony, this firm has reduced the hours of work, and the Clerical Staff will now only have to be present between the hours of 7am and 6pm on week days. The Sabbath is for Worship, but should any Man-of-War or other vessel require victualling, the Clerical Staff will work on the Sabbath.

3 Daily prayers will be held each morning in the Main Office. The Clerical Staff will be present.

4 Clothing must be of a sober nature. The Clerical Staff will not disport themselves in raiments of bright colours, nor will they wear hose unless in good condition.

5 Overshoes and Top-coats may not be worn in the Office, but Neck Scarves and Headwear may be worn in inclement weather.

6 A stove is provided for the benefit of the Clerical Staff. Coal and Wood must be kept in the locker. It is recommended that each member of the Clerical Staff bring four pounds of coal each day during cold weather.

7 No member of Clerical Staff may leave the room without permission from Mr Ryder. The calls of nature are permitted and the Clerical Staff may use the garden below the second gate. This area must be kept in good order.

8 No talking is allowed during business hours.

9 The craving for tobacco, wines or spirits is a human weakness and, as such, is forbidden to all members of the Clerical Staff.

10 Now that the hours of business have been drastically reduced, the partaking of food is allowed between 11.30am and noon, but work will not, on any account, cease.

11 Members of the Clerical Staff will provide their own pens. A new sharpener is available, on application to Mr Ryder.

12 Mr Ryder will nominate a Senior Clerk to be responsible for the cleanliness of the Main Office and the Private Office, and all boys and juniors will report to him 40 minutes before Prayers, and will remain after closing hours for similar work. Brushes, Brooms, Scrubbers and Soap are provided by the Owners.

13 The New increased Weekly Wages are as hereunder detailed:

Junior Boys (to 11 years) 1/4d

Boys (to 14 years) 2/1d

Juniors 4/3d

Junior Clerks 8/7d

Clerks 10/9d

Senior Clerks 21/0d
(after 15 years with the Owners)

THE OWNERS HEREBY RECOGNISE THE GENEROSITY OF THE NEW LABOUR LAWS, BUT WILL EXPECT A GREAT RISE IN OUTPUT OF WORK TO COMPENSATE FOR THESE NEAR-UTOPIAN CONDITIONS.

'The perfect hostess will see to it that the works of male and female authors be properly separated on her bookshelves. Their proximity, unless they happen to be married, should not be tolerated.'

From an 1863 book titled 'Etiquette'

Pearly Gates

There are two types in this world: those who see their very existence as a gamble and play life like a poker machine, furiously feeding superstition into the coin slot in the hope of scoring a jackpot; and those who believe the harder you work, the luckier you get .For both, at the final accounting, there is God—and the prospect of the Pearly Gates.

Letting go is easier said than done. But what better way to say it than with this comforting verse?

Miss Me—But Let Me Go

When I come to the end of the road
And the sun has set for me,
I want no rites in a gloom-filled room,
Why cry for a soul set free?

Miss me a little, but not too long
And not with your head bowed too low.
Remember the love that we once shared.
Miss me—but let me go.

For this is a journey that we must all take
And each must go alone.
It's all part of the Master's plan,
A step on the road to home.

When you are lonely and sick of heart,
Go to the friends we know,
And bury your sorrows in doing good deeds.
Miss me—but let me go.

Swinging Swan Songs

The trouble with funerals is they put the wrong sort of 'dig' into dignity. Someone once advised listeners that from the age of fifty we should not only start auditioning the cast for our inevitable exit, but also produce a show to remember. Music is the key and, according to the Casket Charts, here are the most recent . . .

Top Ten Pearly Greats

1 *Candle In The Wind*, Elton John
2 *Simply The Best*, Tina Turner
3 *My Way*, Frank Sinatra
4 *Knocking On Heaven's Door*, Bob Dylan
5 *Every Step You Take*, The Police
6 *Always Look On The Bright Side Of Life*, Monty Python
7 *Stairway To Heaven*, Led Zeppelin
8 *Always On My Mind*, Elvis Presley
9 *Tears In Heaven*, Eric Clapton
10 *Seasons In The Sun*, Terry Jacks

Not only a funeral favourite but, for many, the most soul-soothing of all final farewells . . .

I Am Not Dead

Do not stand at my grave and weep
For I'm not there, I do not sleep.
I am a thousand winds that blow;
I am diamond glints of snow;
I am the sunlight on ripened grain;
I am the gentle autumn's rain.
When you awaken in the morning's hush;
I am the swift uplifting rush
Of quiet birds encircled flight.
I am the soft star that shines at night.
Do not stand at my grave and cry;
I am not there, I did not die.

Every time I pass a church
I pay a little visit,
So when, at last, I'm carried in
The Lord won't say, 'Who is it?'

Incontrovertible proof that Jesus of Nazareth was a good Jewish boy?: He didn't leave home till he was thirty; He went into his father's business; He believed his mother was a virgin; and she thought that her son was God.

contrib. by Jewish caller

More jokes about—and against—lawyers have been told over talk-back than any other profession. Here's one . . .

A teacher, a garbage collector and a lawyer wound up together at the Pearly Gates. To get into Heaven they had to answer St Peter's question correctly.

First he asked the teacher to name the ship that sank after hitting an iceberg. Having seen the movie, the teacher happily replied 'Titanic!'.

Not relishing the garbo's smell contaminating Heaven, St Peter made his question a bit harder. 'How many people died when the Titanic sank?' '1,513' said the garbo, who also had seen the movie.

St Peter stood aside to let him through the Gates into Heaven. Then he turned to the lawyer. 'Name them all.'

This may be a little sacrilegious, but it shouldn't be left out of the collection. It's reduced too many talkshow hosts to giggles.

Too Much Wholly Spirit

A new priest at his first mass was so scared he could hardly speak. After the service he asked the Monsignor how he had done. 'Fine,' he said, 'But next Sunday it might help if you put a little vodka or gin in your drinking water to relax you.'

The following week the priest added vodka to his water and really kicked up a storm. Once again he asked the Monsignor for an assessment of his performance during the mass.

'Fine,' came the answer. 'But there are a few things you should really get straight . . .

1   There are ten commandments, not twelve.

2   There are twelve disciples, not ten.

3   We do not refer to Jesus Christ as the late JC.

4   Moses parted the water at the Red Sea, he did not pass water.

5   The Pope is consecrated, not castrated, and we don't refer to him as The Godfather.

6   We do not call Judas El Finko.

7   David slew Goliath, he did not kick the shit out of him.

8   And The Father, Son and Holy Ghost are not now and never have been 'Big Daddy, Junior and the Spook'.

Tomorrow

Tomorrow he promised his conscience;
Tomorrow he meant to be good.
Tomorrow I'll do as I ought to,
Tomorrow I'll do as I should.
Tomorrow, tomorrow, tomorrow,
Till youth like a vision was gone;
Till age in his passion had written
A message of faith on his brow.

And forth from the shadows came Death
With the merciless syllable . . . NOW!

I used up all my sick days so I called in dead.

Medical science has now proved you can lengthen your life with laughter. So why not laugh at Death itself?

Good Heavens!

Last night I dreamt that Death came,
And Heaven's gates swung wide,
An angel came with kindly grace
And ushered me inside.

And there, to my astonishment,
Stood folks I'd known on earth,
Some I'd judged as quite unfit,
Others of little worth.

Indignant words rose to my lips
But never were set free.
For every face showed stunned surprise
No-one expected . . . me!

Jesus Who?

An Australian friend was planning to travel to Britain recently. Being a Christian, he reckoned a crucifix on a chain would be a good thing to wear because he's not keen on flying and he felt it would offer a modicum of reassurance. When he requested a crucifix in a jeweller's shop in central Brisbane, the assistant went off to find one and returned saying: 'We have two types. Do you want a plain cross, or one with a little man on it?'

quoted from 'New Scientist'

Where would Christianity be if Jesus had got eight to fifteen years with time off for good behaviour?

N.Y. Senator James Donovan
supporting capital punishment

Dead Unlucky

Legend has it that on the 14th October 1977 the radio station's news director raced into the studio and informed the young man at the mike that, regrettably, Bing Crosby had died.

Before telling the listeners, the presenter dashed to the record library, grabbed a Crosby LP and hurled it onto the turntable.

He then made the sombre announcement, adding, *'As a humble tribute I would like to play you one of his songs'* and immediately followed it with a track picked at random. Unfortunately it was *'Heaven . . . I'm in Heaven . . .'*

A Child's View of God

Passing a church, a five-year-old asked his grandfather 'Who lives there?' His grandfather replied, 'God does.' The child cautiously opened the door to look in, peered through the windows back and front then came to report, 'I couldn't see Him, but I know he's there 'cos his bike's around the back.'

Saint Kev

Before the altar, surrounded by flowers, was the open casket containing Kev, his tattooed arms crossed in repose upon his chest. Kev's wife listened to the eulogy first with sadness, then with mounting amazement. The minister's words were so filled with praise and unbridled admiration for the dear departed, she turned to her young son and said 'Quick! Go down and take a look and make sure it's your dad in that coffin.'

An issue of the 'Brisbane Catholic Leader' has become a collector's item because of this headline on the front page story. It read, **'Men Down Tools for Priesthood'.**

And from a science program: ' . . . a noted mathematician, he died like a recurring decimal sliding off the page . . .'

Cheer up. All is not lost if you believe there are . . .

Just Two Things to Worry About

In life there are only two things to worry about;
Either you are sick, or you are well.

If you're well, there's nothing to worry about.
But if you're sick, there are two things to worry about;
Either you die, or you get well.

If you get well, there's nothing to worry about.
But if you die there are only two things to worry about;
Either you go to Hell, or you go to Heaven.

If you go to Heaven, there's nothing to worry about.
But if you go to Hell . . .
You'll be so bloody busy shaking hands with all your friends you won't have time to worry!

And for those who have absolutely no intention of going unless they can take it all with them: **Hope sees the invisible, feels the intangible and achieves the impossible.**

The Worker's Reward

Last night as I lay sleeping
I died, or so it seems.
And then I went to Heaven.
(But only in my dreams)

And when St Peter met me
Outside the Pearly Gate,
He said, 'I'll get your record,
Please stand here and wait.'

He came back rather flustered,
'Your record's full of flaws.
Didn't you do anything
On earth for a good cause?

'I see here you drank liquor,
And used bad language, too.
Seems that you've done everything
Good folk would never do.

'We can't have your kind up here,
Your life was full of sin.'
Then St Peter's eyes grew large,
He gasped and said, 'Come in!'

He took me to the Big Boss.
'Please treat this sinner well.
It says he worked at _ _ _ _
He's had his share of hell!'

**Possibly the bitter-sweetest four
lines in any treasury:**

The angels blew their trumpets
St Peter said, 'Come'.
The gates of Heaven opened
And in walked Mum.

51

Before radio arrived we could take comfort in Washington Irving's words: 'The grave buries every error, covers every defect, extinguishes every resentment.' Not any more. Speaking ill of the dead is now a career choice. Worse, if your defects are carved in stone they can last for three hundred years or more.

Tombstoned

Sacred to the memory of Anthony Drake,
Who died for peace and quietness sake,
His wife was constantly scolding and scoffing,
So he sought repose in a twelve dollar coffin.

Burlington, Massachusetts

Possibly the best known of all graveyard messages left for posterity is:

Remember me as you pass by
As you are now, so once was I,
As I am now you soon will be,
Therefore prepare to follow me.

Later added: To follow you I'm not content
Until I know which way you went.

Did You Know . . .

In June 1976, to promote more economical use of land set aside for cemeteries, The Melbourne-based Society For Perpendicular Interment launched a worldwide campaign to have people buried upright in cylindrical cardboard coffins?

and . . .

In Canden, Maine, there's a 9 metre high statue over the tomb of Capt. Hanson Gregory who died in 1847? And what great achievement did the statue commemorate? The good Captain put the hole in the doughnut.

Two southern Swedish crematoriums, one in Helsingborg and the other in nearby Boras, are now providing their communities with ten percent of their heating needs and saving up to twelve litres of oil per incineration. Hot air from the furnaces is being piped directly to district energy companies. A spokesman said 'Imagine going home to a nice warm house after the funeral, knowing that Aunt Astrid is heating up the living room'.

Obit. of Fun

My Uncle Fred died of asbestosis. It took six months to cremate him!

On a parish notice board: The cremation of Mr Prendergast will take place at Golders Green Crematorium at 2.30pm.
(added) Please put him on low gas—can't get there till 4.

Notice outside the Metropolitan Tabernacle: The Rev. Charles Spurgeon departed for heaven today at 6.30am.
(added) 10.45am: Not arrived yet. Getting anxious . . . Peter.

It's funny. When you speak to God it's called praying; but when God speaks to you it's called schizophrenia.

Tom Gribble's will stipulated that his body should be cremated and his ashes used for an egg-timer. By being passed down to future generations he could remain a useful member of the family.

'God has a task for each of us, and you just have to do the best you can at it. For me, right now, it just happens to be running a marathon backwards.'

Albert Freese
world backwards marathon record holder

From the Wires:

Under the Contempt of Court Act, alleged murderer Stephen Young was granted a retrial by the judge at the Hove Crown Court, Sussex. The reason? While accommodated overnight at a nearby hotel, some jurors had used a Ouija board to get in touch with the late Harry Fuller, one of the two victims. When juror Ray asked, "Who killed you?" Harry reached out from the ether to spell the message "Stephen Young done it". And, indeed, the new jury found Mr Young guilty.

And from our "Only in America" File:

In the 1980s Californians were offered a unique opportunity to speak to mourners from beyond the grave. It was called The Talking Tombstone. Before going to God, those wishing to leave a permanent message for the bereaved could record their words on a ninety-minute cassette tape. A solar-powered tape recorder built into the tomb would then replay the departed's message each time relatives visited the grave.

A man isn't old when his hair turns grey,
A man isn't old when his teeth decay,
But, buddy, you're in for a very long sleep
When your mind makes appointments your body can't keep.

What happens if you are scared half to death twice?

5 Offspring

All offspring come with a design flaw: they lack an 'off' switch. Happily, so does your love for them, even when they reach that non-stop hormonal Happy Hour called teen age.

A Child's Letter to all Parents

Don't spoil me. I know quite well that I ought not have all the things I ask for. I'm only testing you.

Don't be afraid to be firm with me. I prefer it. It makes me feel secure.

Don't let me form bad habits. I need you to detect them in the early stages.

Don't make me feel smaller than I am. It only encourages me to behave stupidly big. Don't correct me in front of people if you can help it. I'll take more notice if you talk quietly with me in private.

Don't make me feel that my mistakes are sins. This upsets my sense of values.

Don't be hurt when I say I hate you. It isn't you I hate, but the power that you keep using over me.

Don't protect me from consequences. I need to learn the painful way by sometimes facing my mistakes.

Don't take too much notice of my ailments. I'm very good at trading on them.

Don't nag. If you do I shall protect myself by appearing to be deaf.

Don't make rash promises. Remember that I also feel badly let down when promises are broken.

Don't forget that I cannot express myself as well as I should. Learn to read between my lines.

Don't tax my honesty. I'm easily frightened into telling lies.

Don't be inconsistent. This confuses me and makes me lose faith in you.

Don't put me off when I ask questions. If you do I will seek information elsewhere.

Don't tell me my friends are silly. They are real and unique people to me.

Don't ever think it is beneath your dignity to apologise to me. An honest apology makes me feel very warm towards you.

Don't ever suggest that you are infallible. It gives me too big a shock when I find out the truth.

Don't forget that I cannot thrive without lots of your understanding and love. But you already know that.

There are three ways to get something done: do it yourself, employ someone, forbid your children to do it.

There's one home truth every new parent eventually learns: you become free only when your children leave home and the dog dies. Until then you do the best job you can of . . .

Parenting

'I got two As', the small boy said,
his voice was filled with glee.

His father very bluntly asked,
'Why didn't you get three?'

'Mum, I've got the dishes done',
the girl called from the door.

Her mother snapped, 'About time, too.
And did you sweep the floor?'

'I mowed the grass', the tall boy said,
'And put the mower away.'

His father asked him with a shrug,
'Did you clean off the clay?'

*The children in the house next door
seemed happy and content.*

*The same thing happened over there,
but this is how it went:*

'I got two As', the small boy said,
his voice was filled with glee.

His father proudly said, 'It's great
that you belong to me.'

56

'Mum, I've got the dishes done',
the girl called from the door.

Her mother smiled and softly said,
'I couldn't love you more.'

'I mowed the grass', the tall boy said,
'And put the mower away.'

His father answered joyfully,
'How good you've made my day.'

Children deserve a little praise
for tasks they're asked to do.
If they're to lead a happy life,
so much depends on you.

> When talking about or to children, radio presenters require one important quality—sincerity. Once you can fake that you're okay.

Found in a new mum's courtesy pack of infant formula was . . .

Children Learn What They Live

If a child lives with criticism, he learns to condemn.

If a child lives with hostility, he learns to fight.

If a child lives with ridicule, he learns to be shy.

If a child lives with shame, he learns to feel guilty.

If a child lives with tolerance, he learns to be patient.

If a child lives with encouragement, he learns confidence.

If a child lives with praise, he learns to appreciate.

If a child lives with fairness, he learns justice.

If a child lives with security, he learns to have faith.

If a child lives with approval, he learns to like himself.

If a child lives with acceptance and friendship, he learns to find love in the world.

Advertising jingles are now more familiar to children than the old nursery rhymes. But grandparents are on the case. Here's the last verse to the one most requested . . .

The House That Jack Built

This is the farmer sowing his corn,
that kept the cock that crowed in the morn,
that waked the priest all shaven and shorn,
that married the man all tattered and torn,
that kissed the maiden all forlorn,
that milked the cow with the crumpled horn,
that tossed the dog, that worried the cat,
that killed the rat, that ate the malt,
that **lay in the house that Jack built**.

> Familiarity breeds contempt—and children.
>
> *Mark Twain*

> Label on the back of a Batman cape for kids: **For play only. Cape does not enable user to fly.**

Take heart if your cherub was born on a **Wednesday**. Somewhere in the world it was probably a Tuesday or Thursday. Or you could change the spelling to 'whoa'.

Monday's Child

Monday's child is fair of face,
Tuesday's child is full of grace,
Wednesday's child is full of woe,
Thursday's child has far to go,
Friday's child is loving and giving,
Saturday's child works hard for its living,
But the child who is born on the Sabbath day
Is lucky and happy and good and gay.

Diversity

Written and spoken by a 16-year-old girl at the 1997
World Summit of Children

He prayed—it wasn't my religion.
He ate—it wasn't my food.
He spoke—it wasn't my language.
He dressed—it wasn't what I wore.
He took my hand—it wasn't the colour of mine.
But when he laughed—it was how I laughed.
And when he cried—it was how I cried.

From the Wires:

A Senior Educator with the Australian Asthma Foundation was a camp leader in charge of thirty-nine children, including twenty-seven 'very boisterous boys' aged between seven and eleven.

She decided they were so hyped up she'd quieten them down by having a visualisation-meditation session on the floor.

While they were 'floating on a cloud' a small earthquake suddenly shook the ground. The children remained perfectly still. Then afterwards, one small voice piped up, 'How did she do that?'

The Meanest Mother in the World

I have the meanest mother in the world.

While other kids were given lollies for breakfast, kids in my family had to eat cereal, egg and toast.

While other kids had cans of coke and lollies for lunch, I had a sandwich.

As you can guess, when we had meals at home we had to eat ours at a table and not, like all the other kids, in front of the television.

My mean mother also insisted on knowing where we were at all times; you'd think we were on a chain gang or something. She had to know who our friends were, where we were going and even told us what time to be home.

I'm ashamed to admit it, but my mean mother broke child labour laws. She made us work. We had to wash dishes, make our beds and even learn how to cook.

That woman must have stayed up all night thinking up things for us kids to do.

She always insisted we tell the truth, the whole truth and nothing but the truth.

While other kids' mothers bought them brand new bikes and the latest electronic games, our mean mother made us earn and save our pocket money to pay for them.

And by the time we were teenagers, she was making our lives even more unbearable. No tooting the car horn for the girls in our family to come running. Our mean mother embarrassed us by insisting that the boys come to the door to get us.

I forgot to mention that most of our friends were allowed to date at the mature age of 12 and 13. But our old-fashioned mother wouldn't let us date until we were at least 15.

She really raised a bunch of squares. None of us kids was ever arrested for shoplifting or busted for using dope. And who do we have to thank for this? Our mean mother.

Every day we hear cries from people and politicians about what our country really needs. Perhaps what our country really needs are more mean mothers like mine.

Your car comes with a manual. Your teenager doesn't, but should.

Road Report on the Teenager

Suspension—the state in which owners find themselves most of the time.

Brakes—tend to lock when stationary. No effective brake function when connected to sexual, spending or small screen activity.

Steering—periodically deviates from the straight and narrow.

Livery—what owners feel after too many restorative beverages taken during eighteen year running-in period.

Road Holding—varies according to consumption of, usually, someone else's restorative beverage.

Gear Report—constant changing and replacing lead to frequent wearing out . . . mostly of owners' patience and nerves.

Bodywork—high maintenance required. However bulk quantities of hair gel and acne creams fail to remedy hail damage appearance.

Fuel Consumption—higher when stationary than when moving. Fast foods and additives appear to boost performance.

Boot—what owners are tempted to give this model.

The first thing a child learns when they get a drum is that they're never going to get another one.

How many teenagers does it take to make a crowd? One!

Having given your offspring life, the knack is keeping them alive. When the subject cropped up on the open line, callers offered these . . .

Survival Gift Suggestions for Teenagers

- **Hepatitis B immunisation:** it's not called the 'kissing disease' for nothing.

- **A do-it-yourself will kit:** to remind them of their mortality and responsibilities.

- **Juice extractor:** even if used only to make mixers, some nourishment will get through.

- **A year's membership of The Skeptics:** they'll ask questions that could expose the shams and scams.

- **A car/home fire extinguisher and fire blanket:** pop in some spare batteries for the smoke alarm.

- **An advanced defensive driving course:** so they know hotshot drivers don't burn rubber.

- **A book on modern etiquette:** blushes worn with acne is not a good fashion statement.

- **A portable filing system:** efficient bill-paying habits reduce withdrawals from that limitless bank account called Mum and Dad.

- **A first aid kit/course:** first-on-scene life-saving skills can turn even a hooligan into a hero.

- **A no-excuse folder of letter-writing equipment:** containing thank you notelets, stamped envelopes with spare stamps, and a basic selection of greetings cards to cover most occasions.

- **A sober, smart, timeless suit:** think job interviews.

- **A Dial-A-Driver (or local equivalent) gift voucher:** for when they're 'tired and emotional' and need to get themselves and the car home safely.

Do NOT be persuaded to give them:

- Home beer-making equipment, or

- The Complete Indoor Hydroponics Kit.

And a must if they're backpacking overseas:

- **A muggers wallet:** Literally a spare old wallet that'll satisfy a mugger: fill with unusable credit-type cards, US$20 in cash (a small price to pay for survival), useless but official-looking documents and a photo of a pet/old flame/movie star.

- **A travel pouch:** worn next to the body it keeps passport, documents and plastic safe.

- **A reverse charge phone-home facility:** check with your phone company for the latest travellers' service.

- **Travel insurance** that covers all possible disasters.

Forget the fridge magnet. Every family kitchen should display a billboard giving these . . .

Rules of This House

1 If you open it, close it.
2 If you turn it on, turn it off.
3 If you unlock it, lock it.
4 If you break it, repair it.
5 If you can't fix it, call in someone who can.
6 If you borrow it, return it.
7 If you use it, take care of it.
8 If you make a mess, clean it up.
9 If you move it, put it back.
10 If it belongs to someone else and you want to use it, get permission.
11 If you don't know how to operate it, leave it alone.
12 If it doesn't concern you, mind your own business.

It is admirable for a father to take his son fishing, but there's a special place in heaven for the father who takes his daughter shopping.

If you don't want your children to hear what you're saying, pretend you're talking to them.

School exams are designed to reveal where pupils have taken a wrong turn on the path to knowledge. New signposts are advised for the individuals who wrote these . . .

Student Howlers

In Africa they put mosquito nets over the beds to keep out the incest.

A common disease of cereal crops is wheat germ.

The light passes into the eye, through the lens and is focused on the rectum.

Socrates died of an overdose of wedlock.

A sixty-foot tree can break wind for up to 200 yards.

Photo-periodism occurs in animals when they hibernate and shed their leaves.

He spent his days in prison sewing children's balls together.

Martin Luther first came to the historian's eye in 1517 when he nailed his ninety-five faeces to the church door in Wittenburg. (Should be 'theses'.)

When correcting children, speak your words softly and sweetly. Because if your words are soft and sweet they won't taste so bad when you have to eat them.

Cautionary Tales

Cautionary tales may be the parables of the pub, but they do illustrate important lessons, signal warnings and provide the odd bearing for the bewildered. They can tell us, for instance, why people can do considerably more than they think they can, but almost always do considerably less than they think they do. First, some oldies you hadn't remembered you'd forgotten until someone mentioned them on air:

The Sparrow and the Cow

Once upon a time there was a non-conforming sparrow who decided not to fly south for the winter. However, soon the weather turned so cold that he reluctantly had to fly south. In a short time, ice began to form on his wings and he fell to earth in a barnyard almost frozen.

A cow passed by, and crapped on the little sparrow. The bird was sure it was the end for him. But the manure warmed him and defrosted his wings. Cosy and happy, he started to sing.

Just then a large cat came by and, hearing the chirping, investigated the sound. The cat cleared away the manure, found the small, singing bird and promptly ate him.

The moral of the story:

Everyone who craps on you is not necessarily your enemy.

Everyone who gets you out of the crap is not necessarily your friend.

And if you're warm and happy in a pile of crap, keep your mouth shut.

Service Please

Do you remember me? I'm the person who waits patiently for the sales assistant to stop reading the magazine, who stands quietly in line at a shop while counter staff finish their chit-chat, who goes into a restaurant and waits while the waiters do everything but take the order. Yes, I'm the undemanding customer.

But do you know who else I am? I'm the person who never comes back. It's almost amusing to see businesses spending thousands of dollars every year to get me there—when I was there in the first place!

Know When to Quit

A man was in an accident and, even though he was badly hurt, they were able to save his head. They took the head to hospital and put it on a pillow where he lived in relative comfort for many years. Every night he would pray, 'Please God, give me my body back.'

One morning he woke up and was amazed to discover that he had been restored to full health with all his body parts in place. He excitedly grabbed a dressing gown and ran out of the hospital to tell the good news to his mother who lived nearby. As he crossed the road to enter his mother's house, he was run over by a number 9 bus and killed.

The moral of the story:
Quit while you're a head!

Relative Values

A workaholic businessman was in the waiting room of a hospital's Maternity Department. While other expectant fathers paced the carpet and nervously thumbed through magazines, he sat at a table working furiously on a sheaf of papers he had taken from his bulging briefcase.

Eventually a nurse entered the room and spoke to him. 'It's a boy, sir', she announced brightly. 'Well', snapped the businessman without looking up from his work, 'ask him what he wants'.

The original of The Boat Race may be lost to posterity, but this version pretty much makes the same point.

The Boat Race

Once upon a time, Senior Government Management and Private Enterprise decided to have an annual boat race on the city lake. Both teams practised long and hard to reach peak performance, and on the big day they were as ready as they could be.

Private Enterprise won by 50 lengths.

The Government team became very discouraged by the loss, and morale sagged. Senior Government Management resolved to find the reason for the crushing defeat. A project group was set up to investigate and recommend action.

Their conclusion: The problem was that the Private

Enterprise team had eight people rowing and one person steering. The Government team had one person rowing and eight people steering.

Senior Government Management immediately hired a firm of consultants to conduct a study on the team's structure. Millions of dollars and several month's later they concluded that too many people were steering, and not enough rowing.

To prevent another defeat by the Private Enterprise team the Government team structure was changed to two rowers, three steering managers, two senior steering managers and one steering chief executive.

A performance and appraisal system was set up to offer the pair rowing the boat more incentive to work harder. The consultants advised, 'If we give the rowers empowerment and enrichment, that ought to do it'.

The following year the Private Enterprise team won by 100 lengths.

Senior Government Management laid off the rowers for poor performance, sold all the oars, cancelled all capital investment for new equipment, halted research and development on a new boat, awarded high performance bonuses to the consultants and distributed the money saved to members of Senior Government Management.

This caustic communication has featured on bulletin boards since the days of the Telex machine.

Memo: Company Procedure in the Event of Death of an Employee

It has recently been brought to the attention of the Managing Director that employees have been dying while on duty for no apparently good reason. Furthermore, these same employees are failing to fall over after they are dead.

Where it can be proved that the employee is otherwise held up by a bench, counter, desk, typewriter or any other support which is the property of the Department, a 90 day period of grace will be granted.

The following procedure will be strictly adhered to:

If, after several hours, it is noticed that an employee has not moved or changed position, the Department head will promptly investigate. Because of the highly sensitive nature of our staff and the close resemblance between death and their normal work attitude, the investigation will be conducted quietly so as to prevent waking the employee if he or she is merely asleep.

If there is some doubt as to his or her condition, the extending of a pay envelope is an effective test. If the employee does not grasp it, it reasonably can be assumed that he or she is dead.

Note: in some cases, the instinct to extend the hand for the pay envelope is so strongly developed, a spasmodic 'clutch reflex' may occur even after death.

In all cases, a sworn statement by the dead person MUST be filled out in full on a special form provided for this purpose. Fifteen copies will be made, three to be sent to Head Office and two to the deceased. The other copies, in accordance with the usual routine, will be lost in the Departmental filing system.

And another of those malicious little memos with a message for management.

Memo to all Staff

From: Company Secretary

Subject: Early retirement

Due to the economic situation management has decided to reduce the current workforce and has devised a **'Reduction of Employees Program'**. Under this Program older employees will be placed in early retirement, permitting the retention of staff members who represent the future of this company. The Program to phase out personnel aged over 40 by the end of the current financial year will be put into effect immediately. This Program will be known as R.A.P.E., **Retirement of Aged Personnel Early.**

Employees who are R.A.P.E.d will be offered the opportunity to seek other jobs in the company, provided that while they are R.A.P.E.d , they request a review of their status before actual retirement takes place.

This phase of the Program will be known as S.C.R.E.W., **Survey of Capabilities of Retired Early Workers.** All employees who have been R.A.P.E.d and S.C.R.E.W.ed will be able to nominate themselves for a final review.

This phase will be known as s.t.u.f.f.e.d.: **Study of Termination of Use for Further Education and Development.**

Program policy dictates that employees may be r.a.p.e.**d** once, s.c.r.e.w.**ed** twice, but can be s.t.u.f.f.e.d. as many times as management sees fit.

The Old Testament is filled with cautionary tales. Few of them lend themselves to parody more than Noah's Ark . . .

Noah's Lament

And the Lord saith unto Noah,

Where is the ark which I have commanded thee to build? And Noah said unto the Lord,

Verily, I have three carpenters off sick, the supplier hath let me down—yea even though the girder wood hath been on order for nigh on twelve months.

And God saith unto Noah,

I want that ark finished, even after seven days and seven nights.

And Noah said,

Lord, it will be so.

And it was not so.

And the Lord saith,

What seemest to be the trouble this time?

Noah said unto the Lord,

My subcontractor hath gone bankrupt, the pitch which Thou commandeth me to place on the outside and the inside of the ark hath arrived not, and the builder hath gone on strike. And I beseech Thee, Lord, to note that Shem, my son who helpeth me on the ark side of the business, hath formed a pop group with his brothers.

And the Lord grew angry and saith,

Must I chastise thee with whips?

Have you gathered together the unicorns and the fowls of the air?

And Noah wept and said,

Lord, unicorns are a discontinued line, and it hath just been told unto me that the fowls of the air are available only in half-dozens. Lord, thou knowest how it is.

And God in his wisdom saith,

Noah, my son, why else dost thou think I have caused a flood to descend upon the earth?

When a newsroom receives a story that's second or third hand, a Chinese whispers element can affect the accuracy. Somewhat like this vintage tangled tale . . .

The Coming of the Comet

District Telephone Manager to External Plant Manager:

Halley's Comet will soon be visible, an event which occurs only once every 75 years. Have the men meet in the car park at 3 o'clock tomorrow, and I will explain the phenomenon to them and indicate the path the comet will take in the sky above. In case of rain, seat the men in the lunch room and I will show films of the comet.

External Plant Manager to Principal Lines Officer:

By direction of the District Telephone Manager, Halley's Comet will appear above the district at 3 o'clock. If it rains, have the men meet in the lunch room, then take them to the car park where the phenomenon will take place, something which occurs every 75 years.

Principal Lines Officer to Senior Lines Officer:

By direction of the District Telephone Manager, the phenomenal Halley's Comet will appear in the lunch room at 3 o'clock tomorrow. In case it rains, the DTM will order the comet into the car park, as it happens every 75 years.

Senior Lines Officer to Lines Officer:

Tomorrow at 3 o'clock, the District Telephone Manager will appear in the lunch room with the phenomenal Halley's Comet. If it rains, the DTM will give another order, something which occurs every 75 years.

Lines Officer to Linesmen:

When it rains tomorrow at 3 o'clock, the phenomenal 75 year old District Telephone Manager, Mr Halley, will drive his Comet through the lunch room.

Doctors once held a place as the second most trusted professionals in the community. Then doubt set in . . .

Little Doctors

ONE little doctor looks you through and through,
Can't diagnose your case, then there are TWO.

TWO little doctors failing to agree,
Call a consultant, then there are THREE.

THREE little doctors poke you o'er and o'er,
Send for a specialist, then there are FOUR.

FOUR little doctors thinking germs survive,
Phone a pathologist, then there are FIVE.

FIVE little doctors in an awful fix,
Bring in a psychiatrist, then there are SIX.

SIX little doctors when you're nearing heaven,
Fetch a radiologist, then there are SEVEN.

SEVEN little doctors decide to operate,
Call in a surgeon, then there are EIGHT.

EIGHT little doctors think it is your spine,
Ask for a neurologist, then there are NINE.

NINE little doctors, all of them men,
Need a lady doctor, then there are TEN.

TEN little doctors standing by your bed,
Come to a decision and find you are DEAD!

You may have seen the perspicacious Paul Lyneham perform this press preferences list on his 1998 Channel 9 show 'Sex, Lies and Politics'. Being both clever and cautionary it was immediately elevated to radio.

Which Newspapers We Read and Why

- The *Melbourne Age* is read by the people who run the country;
- The *Canberra Times* is read by the people who **think** they run the country;
- The *Sydney Morning Herald* is read by the people who think they **ought** to run the country;
- The *Financial Review* is read by the people who **own** the country;
- The *Melbourne Herald Sun* is read by the **children** of the people who run the country;
- The *Hobart Mercury* is read by the people who think the country ought to be run the way it **used** to be;
- The *Courier Mail* and the *Adelaide Advertiser* are read by the people who think the country **is** run the way it used to be;
- And the *Sydney Telegraph Mirror* is read by the people who don't give a damn **who** runs the country so long as they've got big tits.

Loyalty has its limits, as is suggested in this . . .

Tale of the Tiger

Two men were on a holiday trek through the jungle. Suddenly a native raced past them yelling, 'A tiger's coming, a tiger's coming!' One of the men hastily removed his hiking boots and changed into running shoes. 'Don't be a fool!' called his companion as he stumbled away. 'You'll never outrun a tiger!' 'Wrong, my friend,' came the reply. 'I only have to outrun you.'

If you ever thought engineers were somehow 'different', this piece titled The Duck Theory may confirm it. Faxed anonymously to the studio from a university's psychology department, it obviously made sense to someone.

A COMPARATIVE DISCOURSE

ON THE DIFFERENT TRAINING METHODS

TO BE EMPLOYED FOR

CHILDREN, GEOLOGISTS, DUCKS AND ENGINEERS

It is reasonably assumed that there are only two things harder to train than children. These are geologists and ducks. Engineers are considered totally untrainable and should probably be classified with lemmings.

Children, with little difficulty and only a moderate degree of repetition on the part of a parent or sibling, will soon comprehend the dangers of traffic and display a basic road sense. A four-year-old will not wittingly wander into the path of a rapidly approaching bus or truck.

Geologists and ducks do not commonly display the same awareness, and will develop a small degree of caution only if they survive being run down two or three times. Engineers are unable to comprehend distance and velocity parameters, no matter how often they are hit by a vehicle. In fact, it's not unusual to observe them walking repeatedly into the side of a stationary vehicle based largely on the premise that the obstacle was not there the last time they crossed the road in that location.

A three-year-old child is instinctively computer literate and rapidly grasps the relationship between a TV set and video cassette player, developing a ready aptitude for the complex sequence required to get the Play School tape operating.

It has been stated that the basic difference between a geologist and a computer is that you only have to punch information into a computer once. In this, ducks are somewhat smarter than geologists and also display faster reflexes. Attempting to punch information into a duck usually results in your fist arriving in the space previously occupied by the duck.

Physical force is also futile as a training aid for engineers. If you try to punch information into them they are inclined to develop a fetish and will want to be slapped around at the most inopportune times. It is far easier to tell them gently not to cry, and then turn on the Play School tape for them.

The Cat Farm

Dear Sir,

I'd like to draw your attention to a unique investment opportunity. It is the intention of the our Syndicate to establish a cat farm on land near Dimboola, starting with approximately one million cats.

Each cat produces on average twelve kittens a year and skins can be sold for around 20 cents for black ones, and 40 cents for white ones. This gives a projected first year turnover of $3,600,000, or $72,000 a day.

A qualified Aboriginal cat man can skin up to 1,000 cats per day at a wage of $80. It would take only 50 men to operate the farm, so the gross profits would be around $68,000, or $38,000 net per day.

As the cats would be fed exclusively on rats, and rats multiply four times as fast as cats, our overheads would remain low. We envisage setting up a rat farm adjacent to the cat farm.

If we start with one million rats, that would produce four rats per cat each day. The rats would be fed on the carcasses of the cats that we skin. This will give each rat a quarter of a cat.

As you can see, the business would be self-perpetuating—the cats would eat the rats and the rats would eat the cats and the Syndicate would sell the skins.

Research indicates that we could eventually cross the cats with a readily available species of snake, so they will skin themselves twice a year. Not only will this save labour costs, but it will give us two skins for each cat.

If you would like to join the Syndicate and take advantage of this exciting investment opportunity, I urge you to respond quickly.

Yours truly,

M. Oggy

Born Losers

Someone once explained on air that Americans are by nature optimists because, when the pioneers chased their dream westwards, they discovered fertile valleys. But when early Australians went west they found mostly dust and despondency. Which is why we are more pessimistic, why our humour is more laconic and why short poppies feel an urge to lop rather than laud those who achieve wealth and fame.

The born loser proves that Darwin had a rewind button. If this applies to you, here's . . .

How You Can Tell It's Going to Be a Lousy Day

- You wake up face down in the gutter.
- You put your bra on backwards and it fits better.
- You call Suicide Prevention and they put you on hold.
- You see a '60 Minutes' news crew waiting on your doorstep.
- Your birthday cake collapses under the weight of the candles.
- You want to put on the clothes you wore home from the party last night—but there aren't any.
- You turn on the news and they're showing emergency routes out of the city.
- Your twin sister forgot your birthday.
- You wake up and discover your water bed broke— then you remember you don't have a water bed.
- Your car horn goes off accidentally and remains stuck as you follow a group of Hell's Angels up the freeway.
- Your wife wakes up feeling amorous and you have a headache.
- Your boss tells you not to bother taking off your coat
- The bird singing outside your window is a vulture.

- You walk to work and find your dress is tucked into the back of your pantihose.
- You check in with your answering service and they tell you it's none of your business.
- Your blind date turns out to be your ex-wife/husband.
- Your income tax rebate cheque bounces.
- You put both contact lenses in the same eye.
- Your pet rock snaps at you.
- Your wife says, 'Good morning, Bill' and your name is George.

Life is a grindstone. Whether it grinds us down or polishes us up depends on us.

L. Thomas Holdcraft

The poorest person isn't the one without a cent—it's the one without a dream.

So who are the born losers? They reveal themselves nightly on the open line. Take, for instance, these examples of . . .

Born Loser Logic

Yes, these statements have all been heard on air:

- If it hadn't been for Thomas Edison, we'd be watching TV by candle light.
- How to get your garden well dug for nothing: bury a human skull and call the police.
- The trouble with short astronauts is they start at a lower altitude and cost more in fuel.
- The Brits have to destroy thousands of mad cows. The Cambodians have to get rid of millions of land mines. Why don't they ship the cows to Cambodia and set them loose in the minefields?

Born Loser's Five Reasons for Getting the Sack

1 **Dishonesty**—fiddling the books
2 **Incompetence**—fiddling the books and getting caught
3 **Indiscretion**—letting everyone know that it took four months to find out you were fiddling the books
4 **Gross incompetence**—fiddling the books and ending up out of pocket to the tune of $1,245
5 **Inefficiency**—wanting to fiddle the books, but not knowing where they are

Followed by . . .

Four Ways to Sack a Loser

- Stand the person concerned in his/her own out-tray.
- Send a memo around advising that everyone else in the company will not be sacked with effect from tomorrow.
- Without telling the individual you wish to dismiss, relocate the entire company to Gulargambone overnight.
- Tell him/her that for reasons of national security, he/she will henceforth be working from home without pay.

both lists suggested by Keith Ray's
The Extremely Serious Guide To Business
(1986 Columbus Books, UK)

VOTE 1

The trouble with political jokes is they get elected.

Roosters rule; but to the feather dusters of this world failure can become a way of life:

7 Maxims for Misfits

- Work is for people who don't know how to fish.

- I know you believe you understand what you think I said, but I'm not sure you realise that what you heard is not what I meant.

- People who say failure to prepare is preparing to fail can see what's coming.

- You know your fear of flying is justified when the first word you see at the airport is **terminal**.

- Honesty is the best policy, but insanity is the best defence.

- Eagles may soar, but weasels don't get sucked into jet engines.

- The early bird might get the worm, but it's the second mouse that gets the cheese.

Never forget, Nature sides with the hidden flaw.

And for those with a political bent: politics is like a high mountain. Only eagles and reptiles can get to the top.

Born losers leave evidence: Ian Kearnan, Clean Up Australia founder, tells a tale of a garden gnome fished out of a fouled-up waterway. It had been bound and gagged.

It is possible for a born loser to reverse his/her fortunes. The unappealing and easily ignored aardvark made up the name for himself when he learnt that Noah was going to load the ark in alphabetical order.

Winners vs Losers

A winner always has a solution,
A loser is always part of the problem;

A winner always has a goal,
A loser always has an excuse;

A winner sees answers in every doubt,
A loser sees doubts in every answer;

A winner says it might be difficult, but it's possible,
A loser says it might be possible, but it's too difficult.

You Might As Well Live

Razors pain you

Rivers are damp

Acids stain you

Drugs cause cramp

Guns aren't lawful

Nooses give

Gas smells awful

You might as well live.

poet Dorothy Parker

Movie Losers: a Hint That Death Is Imminent

'Relax. There's no way they can get in now.'

'Oh yes, of course I'll marry you, 007.'

'Hello, operator—I've been cut off. Hello, operator!'

'We'll get out of this place first thing in the morning.'

'Don't worry. You're safe now.'

'Ah ha! So it was you all along!'

'Why are you looking at me like that?'

'Let's split up and I'll search the cellar...'

'Phew. It's only you—come in . . .'

'Why did you bring me all the way up here?'

sourced from the *UK Mail on Sunday, YOU* magazine

Unofficial Parking Ticket

State:...... Registration No: .... Date: ....
Make Of Automobile: .... Time: ...

Unfortunately this is not an official Parking Ticket. But judging from your pathetic and feeble attempt at parking, you deserve to get three.

You, my friend, rank amongst those thick-headed, selfish, inconsiderate drivers who think they and their needs are above everyone else and I trust I will never have the misfortune to share the roads with you again.

The reason for giving you this ticket is so that, in future, you may please learn to park like a civilised person and try to compensate for your obvious multitude of inadequacies in ways that do not inconvenience the rest of us.

Since individuals like yourself probably lack the IQ to understand this message, I sign off wishing you repeated engine failure on remote roads awash with mire, the chill of doubt at each RBT station, and may the fleas of a thousand camels infest your armpits.

With my compliments

And from the newsroom, a selection of international wires that prove some individuals move ever onwards and downwards.

Born Loser Award

Nominee 1

An armed robber holding up a store in Rome (Italy) panicked when police arrived on the scene, and grabbed a bystander as a hostage. He held a gun to the hostage's head and threatened to shoot . . . and the cops fell about laughing. The hostage was a shop window dummy.

Nominee 2

Police were called to break up a brawl during a dominoes tournament in Sunderland (UK), after it was discovered that the winner had used pieces with removable dots.

Nominee 3

Lifeguard Lorenzo Trippi has been sacked after killing three men instead of saving them. Three times in the space of six months while on patrol in Ravenna, Italy, Trippi threw lifebelts to drowning swimmers, but hit them on the head knocking them unconscious.

And the Winner Is . . .

Lille (France) housewife Madame Prelle, who became so fed up with neighbours parking outside her home, after weeks of pleading she arose before dawn one morning and set to work on the gleaming maroon Citroën in front of her gate. Gleefully she scratched the paintwork with a wire brush, poured litres of gloss paint over the roof and slashed the tyres before returning to her bed, deeply satisfied. She was awakened later by her husband who wanted to announce his tenth anniversary present to her . . . a brand new maroon Citroën.

The Hotly Contested S.P.L.A.T.*

*Seriously Pea-Brained Loser of Australia Trophy

This goes, indisputably, to the knife-wielding would-be burglar who broke into a Sydney apartment on 17th March 1999 and found himself face-to-face with the occupants—two hulking Australian National Rugby League front-row forwards. He left the scene by ambulance, wearing a neck brace and an expression of utter terror.

Did you hear about the born loser who tried to buy night-storage solar panels?

A fool and his money are soon popular.

1880 to 1950 was the Golden Age of Futurists Who Fouled Up, people whose predictions were so far off the mark, their fame and forecasts have been recorded for posterity. There's a lot to be said for 20/20 hindsight.

The Golden Age of Futurists Who Fouled Up

'Unworthy of the attention of practical and scientific men.' *Conclusion of a British Parliamentary Committee report on Edison's electric light bulb.*

'Everything that can be invented, has been invented'. *Charles H. Duell, US Commissioner of Patents, 1899.*

'X-Rays will prove to be a hoax.' *Lord Kelvin, President, Royal Society, 1893.*

'Airplanes are interesting toys but of no military value.' *WWI commander Marshal Ferdinand Foch, 1911.*

'Who the hell wants to hear actors talk?' *Harry M. Warner, Warner Brothers, 1927.*

'There is no likelihood that man can ever tap the power of the atom.' *Nobel Prize winner Dr Robert Mullikan, 1923.*

'Stocks have reached what looks like a permanently high plateau.' *Irving Fisher, economics professor, 1929.*

'Believe me, Germany is unable to wage war.' *British Prime Minister David Lloyd George, 1934.*

'Television won't be able to hold on to any market it captures after the first six months. People will soon get tired of staring at a plywood box every night.' *Darryl F. Zanuck, Head of 20th Century Fox, 1946.*

'Computers in the future may perhaps only weigh 1.5 tons.' *Popular Mechanics, 1949.*

And we can't neglect Decca Record's 1962 rejection of a new group called the Beatles: 'We don't like their sound. Groups of guitars are on the way out.' *Nice one!*

For the born loser in love, it seems the more worthy the intention, the more worthless the effort.

The Mix-up

A young man wanted to purchase a gift for his new sweetheart's birthday. After careful consideration he decided on a pair of prettily trimmed dress gloves which he felt would strike just the right note—romantic, but not too personal. Accompanied by his sweetheart's young sister he went to the department store and bought the gloves; at the same time the sister purchased a pair of panties for herself. During the wrapping the shop assistant mixed up the items—the sister got the gloves and the sweetheart got the panties. Without checking the contents, the young man had sealed the package and sent it to his sweetheart along with the following note:

Dearest,

I chose these because I noticed that you are not in the habit of wearing any when we go out in the evening. If it had not been for your sister, I would have chosen the long ones with the buttons, but she wears the short ones which are easier to remove.

These are a delicate shade, but the lady I bought them from showed me a pair which she had been wearing for the past three weeks, and they were hardly soiled. I had her try on yours for me and she looked really smart.

I wish I was there to put them on for you for the first time, as no doubt other hands will come in contact with them before I have a chance to see you again.

When you take them off, remember to gently blow in them before putting them away, as they will naturally be a little damp from wearing. Just think how many times I will kiss them during the coming year. I hope you will wear them for me on Friday night.

All my love . . .

PS: The latest style is to wear them folded down with a little fur showing.

A Few Gems from Personnel Performance Assessment Reports:

"This man is depriving a village somewhere of an idiot."

"He sets low personal standards and consistently fails to achieve them."

"He would be out of depth in a carpark puddle."

"This young woman has delusions of adequacy."

Off the Wall

Phobias, potty punchlines, wacky workplace messages, graffiti—one way or another, they're all off the wall. And they all collect companionably at the bottom of the radio ragbag to be dragged out when the need arises; which, if too many listeners suffer from logophobia or phonophobia, it probably does. Frequently.

Graffiti has been the medium of the masses for over 3,000 years. Perhaps the first person to scribble 'graffiti should be obscene and not heard' hadn't heard of talkback.

Top Ten Masonry Messages

1   In the beginning was the word, and the word was AARD-VARK.

2   To do is to be .... Rousseau
    To be is to do .... Sartre
    Dobedobedo .... Sinatra

3   Back in a minute ..... Godot

4   I like sadism, necrophilia and bestiality: am I flogging a dead horse?

5   Psychology is producing habits out of a rat.

6   Tutankhamun has changed his mind and wants to be buried at sea.

7   Say it with flowers—give her a triffid.

8   I'd rather have a full bottle in front of me, than a full frontal lobotomy.

9   VENI, VECI, VD

10 O.O..O.O..A.Q.I.C...I.8.2.Q..B.4.I.P

This one defies comment . . .

Don't throw your fag ends in the loo,
You know it isn't right.
It makes them very soggy
And impossible to light.

How I wish I were what I was when I wished I were what I am . . .

Disembowelling takes guts!

Not so easy to convey over radio, but still appreciated:

Graffiti Rules Okay

- Dyslexia lures, KO
- Synonyms govern, all right
- Roget's Thesaurus dominates, regulates, rules, OK, adequately, stamp of approval . . .
- Irish drama rules, O'Casey
- Nostalgia rules, Hokey-Cokey
- Jargon rules, ongoing agreement situation
- Flower power rules, bouquet
- James Bond rules, OOK
- Morse Code rules, . . . —
- The King of Thailand rules Bangk, OK
- Scots rule, och aye
- Bureaucracy rules, OK
                      OK
                      OK
- Democracy rules,   OK   40%
                      NO   35%
          Don't know 25%

Scrawled under a street sign saying **Avenue Road**— what's wrong with the old one, then?

And that mortar-fying message with timeless appeal: constipation is the thief of time, diarrhoea waits for no man.

Some of the most telling texts are found on workplace walls.

That's Not My Job

This is the story about four people named **everybody**, **somebody**, **anybody** and **nobody**.

There was an important job to be done, and **everybody** was sure **somebody** would do it. **Anybody** could have done it, but **nobody** did it.

Somebody got angry about that, because it was **everybody**'s job.

Everybody thought **anybody** could do it, but **nobody** realised that **everybody** wouldn't do it. It ended up that **everybody** blamed **somebody** when **nobody** did what **anybody** could have done.

Doing a good job around here is like wetting your pants in a dark suit. It gives you a warm feeling but nobody notices.

Notice

This department requires no physical fitness program. Everyone gets enough exercise jumping to conclusions, flying off the handle, running down the boss, knifing friends in the back, pushing their luck, dodging responsibility, passing the buck and chasing their tails.

For Immediate Attention of Staff

Due to escalating costs, increased competition and a keen desire to stay in business, we have found it necessary to introduce a new policy. Effective immediately, it is required that some time between starting time and quitting time, and so as not to interfere too much with lunch periods, smokos, coffee breaks, calls of nature and discussions of last night's TV programs, each employee will find time for what we shall call . . .

The Work Break!

Let It Be Known

We, the unwilling,
led by the unknowing,
are doing the impossible
for the ungrateful.
We have done so much for so long with so little
we are now qualified to do anything.

Another month ends.
All targets met.
All systems working.
All customers satisfied.
All staff eager to meet new challenges.
All pigs fed and ready to fly.

A heckler on the line can be a gift.
That's when you'll hear those
pithy . . .

Presenter Put-downs

- If Moses had known you, there would have been another Commandment.

- You have a ready wit. Let me know when it's ready.

- I'd put a curse on you, but somebody's beaten me to it.

- I'm not going to engage in a battle of wits with you. I never attack an unarmed man.

. . . (265 if you include arachibutyrophobia, the fear of getting peanut butter stuck to the roof of the mouth), each with its own name. Fears are not phobias. The most common adult fear is public speaking; and for children it's being left alone. Some phobias are well-named: dikephobia—fear of the law, gametophobia—fear of marriage, gymnophobia—fear of nudity, potophobia—fear of drink, thaasophobia—fear of sitting idly and pantophobia—fear of everything. But if these don't appeal to you, perhaps you'll find something that suits in the following . . .

Phascinating Phobias

beards	phgonophobia
being buried alive	taphephobia
being stared at	scopophobia
being touched	aichmophobia
blushing	erythrophobia
body odour	bromidrosiphobia
clowns	coulrophobia
crossing bridges	gephyrophobia
dawn	eosophobia
doctors	iatrophobia
dust	koniophobia
empty beer glass	zymocenosilicaphobia
flutes	aulophobia
fog	homichlophobia
going to bed	clinophobia
gold	aurophobia
gravity	barophobia
heaven	ouranophobia
home	oecophobia/oikophobia
imperfection	atelophobia
infinity	apeirophobia
knees	genuphobia
looking in the mirror	spectrophobia
magic	rhabdophobia
mirrors	eisoptrophobia
missiles	ballistophobia
money	chrometophobia

monsters	teratophobia
needles	belonephobia
passing high buildings	batophobia
phobias	phobophobia
pins	enetophobia
railways	siderodromophobia
relatives	syngenescophobia
responsibility	hypegiaphobia
ridicule	katagelophobia
rust	iophobia
saints	hagiophobia
shadows	sciophobia
sin	hamartophobia
sitting down	kathisophobia
slime	blennophobia
standing upright	stasiphobia
stooping	kyphophobia
string	linonophobia
symmetry	symmetrophobia
teddy bears	arctophobia
thinking	phronemophobia
vomiting	emetophobia
wealth	chrematophobia
work	ergophobia
worms	helminthophobia

For most kitchen comedians the open line is the only place they can perform safely and anonymously to a large, if not always rapt, audience.

Switchboard Seinfelds Said . . .

- *you can lead a horse to water but you can't force rhubarb.*

- **we need canals. It's the only way to keep prostitutes off the street.**

- *well, actually he put rhino dung on the rhubarb. It grew wonderfully, but you need a shotgun to kill the greenfly.*

- she was so thin I thought she was a pool cue. Before I knew it I'd chalked her and got a break of 46.

- *yeah, we tried that once, but couldn't use the fan for months afterwards.*

- he's wealthy, but uncomfortable; that's the trouble with piles of gold.

- *she's had her face lifted so many times she has to shave her chin.*

- I don't understand all the fuss about adult illiterates. Let them take a correspondence course.

- *look, if I wanted to hear more, I'd buy a bag of the stuff and spread it under the roses.*

- I asked him if he had any dogs going cheap and he said no, all our dogs go woof.

Every talkback program has its unofficial club of conspiracy theory callers. Members feverishly swap data and developments and dismiss those who mock as being too trusting or part of the conspiracy. To them, charting the contours of catastrophe is a crusade. But as far as the rest of us are concerned,

We Don't Wish to Know That . . .

Next time a giant asteroid is hurtling earthwards, we'll be the last to know.
True, as of May 1998 when NASA and international astronomers decided to keep news of future potential apocalyptic collisions to themselves for at least 72 hours, enough time to review their calculations and synchronise their joint statements with evening TV news broadcasts.

An overdose of female hormones in our environmental waste is threatening the human male sperm count and survival of other species. Humanity hoist by its own P.E.T.ard? Latest research indicates one culprit is phthalate used in soft PVC plastic.

We are living in a dangerous electronic soup.
Some experts may warn us that electromagnetic radiation from modern technology could prove cell-damaging but, be honest, could you cope without a mobile phone, ATM, personal computer, microwave oven, VCR . . . ?

Chemical food additives, irradiation and genetic engineering may have a long-term hazardous effect on human health.
What can we say? Only time and the odd mutant will tell; because vested interests certainly won't. And those strawberry-flavoured sprouts taste great!

The mercury in our amalgam fillings is poisoning us.
If shown to be true, the bullion-busting lawyers-versus-dentists stoush will delight tabloid TV and talkshow broadcasters who, as we speak, are having their fillings replaced.

Fluoride, aluminium and other chemicals added to our tap water are attacking our immune systems.
Could be. But the good news is our longevity has increased to around 80 years and the spring water industry is booming.

We've consumed so many antibiotics we now have little protection from lethal bacteria picked up in hospitals.
Possibly, admits the medical profession. But look on the bright side. At least it'll shorten the public hospital waiting lists.

Serious crime is so rife we'll all be murdered in our beds.
Fear not; the per capita murder rate in Australia is the same as 100 years ago. The most significant crime rise is in drug-related robberies.

There's a US government-lead global conspiracy to conceal the fact that extra-terrestrials have visited earth.
Could it be a desperate attempt by aliens to make sure we don't contaminate the rest of the galaxy with our nasty habits?

Powerful oil and coal corporations are not only preventing the development of cheap renewable energy, some are actively promoting the benefits of the greenhouse effect.
Sadly, propaganda material distributed by some major firms involved in non-renewable energy suggests there could be a degree of truth in this.

To establish a new world order and challenge the independence of economically healthy nations like Australia the World Bank, the IMF and the Fabians are plotting to disarm citizens and subjugate everyone to a totalitarian world government.
Er . . . we are talking about those savvy organisations that failed even to anticipate the 1998 Asian market crash?

Four Off-the-Wall Wires:

To circumvent animal rights campaigners, the American fur industry has produced a real fur coat that looks like a fake.

A Russian company has developed glasses with holographic images of wide-open eyes for executives or government officials who want to appear alert while dozing at meetings.

Sado-masochists in the Netherlands have demanded special fire safety measures in brothels, including pliers to cut handcuffs.

The Northrop Corporation of America, makers of the B-2 Stealth bomber, has gone to law to stop a condom manufacturer using the trademark 'Stealth', on the grounds that having the same name for an aircraft bomber and a condom was 'likely to cause confusion'.

On the morning of her sixteenth birthday, a teenager awoke to find this message from her Mum at the foot of her bed, pinned to the cluttered corkboard among all the school exam schedules and photos of movie and pop stars.

To My Daughter

I gave you life, but I cannot live it for you.
I can teach you things, but I cannot make you learn.
I can give you directions but I cannot be there to lead you.
I can allow you freedom, but I cannot account for it.

I can take you to church, but I cannot make you
 believe.
I can teach you right from wrong, but I cannot always
decide for you.
I can buy you beautiful clothes, but I cannot make
 you beautiful inside.
I can offer you advice, but I cannot accept it for you.

I can give you love, but I cannot force it upon you.
I can encourage you to share, but I cannot make you
 unselfish.
I can teach you respect, but I cannot force you to
 show honour.
I can advise you about friends, but I cannot choose
 them for you.

I can discuss sex with you, but I cannot keep you pure.
I can explain the facts of life, but I cannot build your
 reputation.
I can tell you about drink, but I cannot say 'no' for you.
I can alert you to the dangers of drugs, but I cannot
 prevent you from using them.

I can describe lofty goals, but I cannot achieve them
 for you.
I can teach you kindness, but I cannot insist that you
 be gracious.
I can warn you aboout sin, but I cannot make you moral.
I can give you unconditional love all of my life . . .
 And I will!
 Always,

 Mum

94

Between the Lines

As anyone in commerce, government and even education knows, there's often a yawning chasm between what's stated officially, and what's really meant. It doesn't take a cryptographer to get a grasp on gobbledegook. All you need is an unofficial glossary of terms . . .

We'll start with the . . .

Basics of Industry Terminology

Please treat this in the strictest confidence
Tell one person at a time.

I have good reason to believe . . .
I'm guessing.

The grapevine tells me . . .
I hope.

The industry's view is . . .
A company made up of one man, his dog and BMW thinks.

This is a progressive, commercially viable company . . .
They give good lunches.

This company is an industry leader . . .
They give good dinners.

This is an interesting and thought-provoking proposal . . .
I don't understand it.

This proposal is well thought out . . .
I do understand it.

This expenditure should be examined by an accountant . . .
The figures don't add up.

I can confidentally approve this expenditure . . .
The figures do add up.

Seasonally adjusted analysis shows . . .
I've doctored the figures.

There is no historical data . . .
I've lost the file.

Significant effort will be required to process this case . . .
I've done something very clever and I want everyone to know.

The interlineally literate (those who can read between the lines) will immediately recognise this . . .

Explanation of Departmental Phraseology

Your enquiry is being looked into:
We haven't even read your letter.

We will look into the problem:
Give it a couple of weeks and we hope you'll forget about the whole thing.

We will advise you in due course:
Once we have some idea of what we're talking about, we'll let you know.

We are aware of the situation:
We have lost the file.

The matter is under consideration:
We've never even heard of it.

The matter is under urgent consideration:
We are looking in the rubbish bin for your letter.

We are undertaking a study:
We need a month to think of an excuse.

I think we can work together on this:
When you've worked out what the problem is we hope you'll let us know.

Please note and initial:
It's not my problem now.

Please give us your interpretation:
We've already made our decision so your opinion is worth bugger-all.

Let us discuss the matter further:
I'll meet you down the pub.

To assist with further decoding, we offer this . . .

Glossary of Management Jargon

Delegate: pass the buck

Delegate upwards: pass the buck back

Filed: lost

Pending: what the hell do we do with this?

Delayed: forgotten

Urgency: panic

Extreme urgency: blind panic

Frank and open discussion: blazing row

Analytical projection: guess

Long range forecast: wild guess

Scheduled: hoped for

Deficiency analysis: pointing the finger

Ambitious: ruthless

Strategy: low cunning

Shrewd: devious

Profit: profit

Profit before tax: loss

Deficit: staggering loss

Industrial by-product: our waste

Environmental pollution: other people's waste

Supplementary statistical information: padding

New: last year's model in a different colour

Adverse consumer reaction: the boss's wife didn't like it

Ingeniously engineered: incredibly difficult to install and service

Exhaustive tests: the sales manager took it home to his kids

Tested to destruction: the sales manager's kids broke it

The Lewis Carroll School of R&D Reporting

Did not operate as well as predicted . . .
It burst into flames.

If instability results, appropriate remedial action will suggest itself . . .
If instability results, you'll have to think of something fast, Jack!

The equation was solved numerically . . .
We averaged eight different answers.

This value is a first approximation . . .
This value is flagrant guesswork.

Some reservations should be placed on these figures . . .
These figures are bloody useless.

There are certain practical difficulties in realising the gain assessments . . .
All the transistors burnt out simultaneously.

It can be construed that . . .
Any guess is valid.

According to the Nuttall's Standard Dictionary, 'sophisticated' means 'deprived of simplicity'. Which brings us to the most sophisticated jargon of all:

Translating Officialese

Procedural safeguard.
Red tape.

Data emanating from source is impacting suboptimally in the catchment area.
Nobody understands it.

Conditional upon the continuation of current economic variables.
If pigs fly.

Implement an inbuilt visibility reduction strategy in the dissemination of data.
Create a smokescreen.

Interpreting That School Report

Satisfactory progress: I can't think of a single interesting thing about him/her.

A born leader: Runs a protection racket.

Easy going: Bone idle.

Lively: Thoroughly disruptive.

A sensitive child: Never stops whining.

Helpful: Creep.

Reliable: Grasses on his mates.

Adventurous: Will break his neck before the year's out.

Has difficulty forming relationships: I can't stand him either.

Expresses himself confidently: Cheeky little bastard.

Enjoys all PE activities: Thug.

Has had a lot of minor illnesses: Bunks off regularly.

Friendly: Never shuts up.

Works better in a small group: Daren't take my eyes off him/her for a second.

Imaginative: Lies and cheats frequently.

Needs praise and encouragement: Thick as two short planks.

Expresses himself clearly: Foul mouthed.

Does not accept authority easily: Dad's doing time.

Is easily upset: Is spoilt rotten.

Often appears tired: Stays up till all hours watching horror movies or glue sniffing.

Works better at practical activities: Totally illiterate.

Good with his hands: Light fingered.

A rather solitary child: Smells or has nits.

Independent-minded: Obstinate.

Enjoys extracurricular activities: Flogs cigarettes.

Determined: Completely lacking all scruples.

A good sense of humour: Teases other kids unmercifully.

Popular at Play Centre: Sells pornography.

A vivid imagination: Never short of an excuse.

An inquisitive mind: Often caught playing Doctors and Nurses.

Does not give classes his full attention: Smokes in the lavatory.

Chooses his friends carefully: National Front.

Diagnosing Specialist-speak

What the Doctor Says/What the Doctor Means

Well, well, well, what have we here?
I haven't the faintest idea what's wrong with this poor little bugger!

We should take care of this straight away.
I need some extra cash to pay for my golf clubs.

Let's first check your medical history.
I wonder if this little creep paid his last bill.

Can we make an appointment for later in the week?
I wish you'd nick off. My golf starts at three.

No I wouldn't really recommend a second opinion.
Why should I let those mongrels rake in more money?

We've got some good news and some bad news.
We've amputated the wrong leg, but we got a good price for your carpet slippers.

Let's see how it develops.
Maybe it'll grow into something we can cure.

I'd like to prescribe a new drug.
I get paid by the drug company for each guinea pig I can book.

This might hurt a little.
The last two patients bit their tongues off before they fainted.

Yes, there's a lot of it going around at the moment.
That's the fifth case this week. I'd better find out what it is before I get it too.

Insurance firms covering motorists have databases bulging with bizarre explanations of how the vehicle came to be damaged. Many are . . .

Stranger Than Fiction

- Coming back, I took the wrong turning and drove into a tree that wasn't there.
- **I was having an argument with my wife. She pulled my hair causing me to turn into a lamp standard.**
- I leant forward to swat a bee on the windscreen and hit the car in front.
- **I collided with a stationary truck coming the other way.**
- A pedestrian hit me and went under my car.
- **A cow wandered into my car. I was afterwards informed the cow was half-witted.**
- I thought the side window was down but it was up, as I found out when I put my head through it.
- **I left my Mazda ute outside the bank for a few minutes and when I came out it had turned into a Ford ute.**
- The other driver was all over the road. I had to swerve a number of times before I eventually hit him.
- **In an attempt to stop myself sneezing, I turned into a caravan.**
- I had been driving for fifty years when I fell asleep at the wheel and drove into the ditch.
- **I was rear-ended while driving my father to work. I was turning on the car radio when my dad yelled 'Stop!'. So I did. But the voice was from the radio, not my dad.**

Few communications come more garbled than . . .

Notes to the Milkman

'No milk today. When I say today, I mean tomorrow because I wrote this note yesterday.'

'No milk today thank you. We are away for the weekend which is why I am hiding this note under the doormat so nobody finds out.'

'I cannot pay all of this month's bill today as my husband died last Monday. I will give you the remains next week.'

'Do not leave any milk next door as he is dead until further notice.'

You have to be smart to reduce complex systems of government and laws of economics to a couple of lines. But someone's done it.

You Have Two Cows

Communist: You have two cows. The state takes both and sells you the milk.

Socialist: You have two cows. The state gives one to your neighbour and sells you both the milk.

Dictatorship: You have two cows. The state shoots you, and takes both cows.

Capitalist: You have two cows. You sell the milk and buy a bull.

And what exactly are those two famous laws?

Parkinson's Law: That work expands to fill the time available to do it. Or that the amount of work varies inversely to the number of people employed.

Cyril Northcote Parkinson 1958

Peter Principle: That in every organisation every employee rises to the level of their own incompetence. All valuable work is therefore done by people who have not yet reached that level.

Prof. Laurence J. Peter 1966

One particular catchphrase that's often misused on air is . . .

Catch 22

Comes from the book of the same name by Joseph Heller and is a code word for no-win absurdity. When exhausted American aircrew members desperate to stop flying dangerous missions over enemy territory tried to plead insanity, they were instantly assessed as sane and ordered to keep flying. After all, only an insane person would choose to keep putting his life in such danger. As soon as they wished to stop flying they must, therefore, be judged sane.

You won't have to look between the lines for the words that really count . . .

The Most Important Words of All

The six most important words: I admit I made a mistake.

The five most important words: You did a good job.

The four most important words: What is your opinion?

The three most important words: If you please.

The two most important words: Thank you.

The least important word: I.

'Scott, would you like some more alphabet soup'
'No thanks mum, I couldn't eat another word.'

You can learn some intriguing facts of life by studying TV dramas and movies . . .

- A detective can only solve a case once he's been sacked.

- You throw away the gun when you run out of bullets.

- No matter how heavy the traffic, a parking space will always be available outside any building about to be entered.

- If you start singing and dancing in the street, anyone who happens to be near you will know the words and steps and readily join in.

- All good guys throughout history, even medieval peasants, had perfect teeth.

- Nubile slave girls in Biblical times routinely waxed their legs and bikini-lines and wore false eyelashes.

The sign in the barber's shop window says "Haircuts While You Wait". Hmmmm . . .

10 Philosophies

Homespun philosophy and late night talkback were made for each other. Where else would you hear 'we are the people our parents warned us about' and 'have humming birds forgotten the words?' And where else could you bask in the glow of old friends such as 'Desiderata' and 'Footprints In The Sand'?

Desiderata

Go placidly amid the noise and haste and remember what peace there may be in silence.

As far as possible, without surrender, be on good terms with all persons. Speak your truth quietly and clearly and listen to others, even the dull and ignorant; they too have their story.

Avoid loud and aggressive persons, they are vexations to the spirit.

If you compare yourself with others, you may become vain and bitter; for always there will be greater and lesser persons than yourself.

Enjoy your achievements as well as your plans.

Keep interested in your own career, however humble; it is a real possession in the changing fortunes of time.

Exercise caution in your business affairs; for the world is full of trickery but let this not blind you to what virtue there is; many persons strive for high ideals; and everywhere life is full of heroism.

Be yourself.

Especially do not feign affection.

Neither be cynical about love; for in the face of all aridity and disenchantment, it is perennial as the grass.

Take kindly the counsel of the years, gracefully surrendering the things of youth.

Nurture strength of spirit to shield you in sudden misfortune but do not distress yourself with imaginings. Many fears are born of fatigue and loneliness.

Beyond a wholesome discipline, be gentle with yourself. You are a child of the universe, no less than the trees and the stars; you have a right to be here, and whether or not it is clear to you, no doubt the universe is unfolding as it should.

Therefore be at peace with God, whatever you conceive God to be, and whatever your labours and aspirations.

In the noisy confusion of life, keep peace with your soul. With all its sham, drudgery and broken dreams, it is still a beautiful world.

Be careful.

Strive to be happy.

> Found in old St Paul's church,
> Baltimore. Dated 1692

Footprints in the Sand

One night a man had a dream. He dreamt he was walking along the beach with the Lord. Across the sky flashed scenes from his life. For each scene he noticed two sets of footprints in the sand. One belonged to him and the other to the Lord.

When the last scene of life flashed before him, he looked back at the footprints in the sand. He noticed that, many times along the path of his life, there was only one set of footprints.

He also noticed that it happened at the very lowest and saddest times in his life. This really bothered him, And he asked the Lord about it.

'Lord, you said once I decided to follow you, you would walk with me all the way. But I have noticed that during the most troublesome times of my life there is only one set of footprints. I don't understand why, in the times when I needed you most, you should leave me.'

The Lord replied, 'My precious, precious child. I love you and I would never leave you during your times of trial and suffering. When you saw one set of footprints, it was then that I carried you'.

Stay tuned and you'll notice there are two types. Those who believe we're born naked, wet and hungry, and things go downhill from there. And those for whom . . .

Life Is Mostly Froth and Bubble

Question not, but live and labour
Till yon goal be won,
Helping every feeble neighbour,
Seeking help from none;
Life is mostly froth and bubble,
Two things stand like stone,
Kindness in another's trouble,
Courage in your own.

Adam Lindsay Gordon (1833–70)

They tell us the World Wide Web has wiped away all national borders and Netizens now belong to a global village. But rest assured, listeners' stamped self-addressed snail mail will continue to womble in whenever these four mini-masterpieces are read out over the air.

To Remember Me

The day will come when my body will lie upon a white sheet neatly tucked under the four corners of a mattress located in a hospital busily occupied with the living and dying.

At a certain moment, a doctor will determine that my brain has ceased to function and that, for all intents and purposes, my life has ceased.

When that happens, do not attempt to instill artificial life into my body by the use of a machine, and don't call this my 'death bed'. Let it be called 'the bed of life', and let my body be taken from it to help others lead fuller lives.

Give my sight to the man who has never seen a sunrise, a baby's face or love in the eyes of a woman.

Give my heart to a person whose own heart has caused nothing but endless days of pain.

Give my blood to the teenager who is pulled from the wreckage of his car, so that he might live to see his grandchildren play.

Give my kidneys to one who depends on a machine to exist from week to week.

Give my bones, every muscle, every fibre and nerve in my body and find a way to make a crippled child walk.

Explore every corner of my brain. Take my cells if necessary, and let them grow so that, some day, a speechless boy will shout at the crack of a bat, and a deaf girl will hear the sound of rain against her window.

Burn what is left of me and scatter the ashes to the wind to help the flowers grow.

If you must bury something, let it be my faults, my weaknesses and all prejudice against my fellow man.

Give my sins to the devil. Give my soul to God.

If, by chance, you wish to remember me, do it with a kind deed or word to someone who needs you.

If you do all that I have asked, I will live forever.

attrib: USA Circuit Court Judge Jacob M. Broad

All I Ever Needed to Know I Learned in Kindergarten

Most of what I really need to know about how to live, and what to do, and how to be, I learned in kindergarten. Wisdom was not at the top of the graduate school mountain, but was there in the sandbox at nursery school.

These are the things I learned: Share everything. Play fair. Don't hit people. Put things back where you found them. Clean up your own mess. Don't take things that aren't yours. Say sorry when you hurt somebody. Wash your hands before you eat. Flush. Warm cookies and cold milk are good for you. Live a balanced life. Learn some, think some, and draw and paint and sing and dance and play and work some every day.

Take a nap every afternoon. When you go out in the world watch for traffic, hold hands and stick together. Be aware of wonder. Remember the little seed in the plastic cup. The roots go down and the plant goes up and nobody really knows why, but we are all like that.

Goldfish and hamsters and white mice and even the little seed in the plastic cup—they all die; and so do we.

And then remember the book about Dick and Jane and the first word you learned, the biggest word of all: LOOK.

Everything you need to know is in there somewhere. The Golden Rule and love and basic sanitation, ecology and politics and sane living.

Think of what a better world it would be if we all— the whole world—had cookies and milk at about 3 o'clock every afternoon and then lay down with our blankets for a nap; or if we had a basic policy in our nation, and other nations, always to put things back where we found them and to clean up our own messes.

And it is still true, no matter how old you are, when you go out in the world it is best to hold hands and stick together.

attrib: Robert Fulghum,
'Kansas City Times', Sept. 17th 1986

Abraham Lincoln Said . . .

You cannot bring about prosperity by discouraging thrift.

You cannot strengthen the weak by weakening the strong.

You cannot help the wage earner by pulling down the wage payer.

You cannot further the brotherhood of man by encouraging class hatred.

You cannot help the poor by destroying the rich.

You cannot establish sound security on borrowed money.

You cannot keep out of trouble by spending more than you earn.

You cannot build character and courage by taking away man's initiative and independence.

You cannot help men permanently by doing for them what they could, and should, do for themselves.

Chief Seattle's Message to the American Congress

The Great Chief in Washington sends word that he wishes to buy our land.

The Great Chief also sends us words of friendship and goodwill, this is kind of him since we know he has little need of our friendship in return.

But we will consider your offer, we know that if we do not sell, the white men might come with guns and take our land.

How can you buy and sell the sky?

The warmth of the land?

The idea is strange to us.

If we do not own the freshness of the air and the sparkle of the water, how can you buy them?

Every part of this earth is sacred to people. Every shining pine needle, every sand shore, every mist in the dark woods, every clearing and humming insect is holy in the memory and experience of my people. The sap which courses through the trees carries the memories.

The white man's dead forget the country of their birth when they go to walk among the stars.

Our dead never forget this beautiful earth, for it is the mother of the red man, we are part of the earth and it is part of us.

Some philosophies touch a nerve, some touch a chord.

If I Had My Life to Live Over

I'd like to make more mistakes next time.

I'd relax. I'd limber up.

I would be sillier than I have been this trip.

I'd take more chances,

I'd climb more mountains, and swim more rivers.

I'd eat more ice cream and less beans.

I would, perhaps, have more actual troubles, but fewer imaginary ones.

I'm one of those people who lived sanely and sensibly, hour after hour, day after day.

Oh, I've had my moments, and if I had to do it over again I'd have more of them.

In fact, I'd try to have nothing else;

just moments, one after the other, instead of living so many years ahead of each day.

I never went anywhere without a thermometer, a hot water bottle, a raincoat and a parachute.

I'd travel much lighter next time,

If I had my life to live over.

I would start barefoot earlier in the spring, and stay that way later in the fall.

I'd go to more dances; I would ride more merry-go-rounds.

I would pick more daisies,

If I had my life to live over.

attrib: Nadine Stair, aged 83, from Louisville, Kentucky

The Gift

It is the *spirit* in which the gift is rich,
As the gifts of the Wise Ones were;
We are not told whose gift was gold,
Or whose was the gift of myrrh.

The key to knowing what you want, is knowing what you must give up before you get it.

If you long for an antidote to all those cynical car bumper stickers that say things like 'Get Lost, I Have Enough Friends' and 'Get In, Sit Down, Shut Up and Hang On', try . . .

The Ten Commandments of Humanity

1 *Speak to people:* there is nothing so pleasing as a cheerful word of greeting.

2 *Smile at people:* it takes seventy-two muscles to frown, only fourteen to smile.

3 *Call people by their name:* the sweetest music to anyone's ears is the sound of their own name.

4 *Be friendly and helpful:* if you would have friends, be a friend.

5 *Be cordial:* speak and act as if everything you do is truly a pleasure.

6 *Be genuinely interested in people:* you can like almost everybody if you try.

7 *Be generous with praise:* and be cautious with criticism.

8 *Be considerate of others' feelings:* there are usually three sides to a controversy: Yours, the other fellow's and the right side.

9 *Be alert to give service:* what counts most in life is what we do for others.

10 *Add to this . . .* a good sense of humour, a big dose of patience and a dash of humility, and you will be rewarded many-fold:

When it comes to giving, some people stop at nothing.

The great thing about having power is you get to put the good guys on the ladders, and the bad guys on the snakes.

For professional talkers, proverbs make good points of reference. They also put a stamp of credibility on universal suspicions.

Ten Modern Proverbs

1 He who laughs last probably is the one who intended to tell the story himself a little later.

2 Introduce some mind over matter into your life. If you don't mind, it doesn't matter.

3 Opportunity knocks only rarely, but temptation bangs on the door for years.

4 It's easy to see through people who make a spectacle of themselves.

5 Better to be silent and be thought a fool than to speak and remove all doubt.

6 The pecking order is strictly for the birds.

7 The only thing worse than being old and bent is being young and broke.

8 The big guns of business are usually those who have never been fired.

9 You'll never lead the band if you can't face the music.

10 Great minds discuss ideas, average minds discuss events, little minds discuss people.

Another old friend . . .

A Prayer

God, grant me the *Serenity*
to accept things I cannot change,
Courage to change the things I can
And *Wisdom* to know the difference.

That roses have thorns is a problem. That thorns have roses is a miracle.

What are the most basic desires and values which drive us all? According to a 1998 survey conducted by Prof. Stephen Reiss of the Ohio State University, here (in no particular order) are our most important . . .

Universal Human Needs

Seeking company and friendship.

The wish to organise our lives.

Avoidance of being neglected.

The desire to avoid pain and anxiety.

The wish for vengeance and desire to take revenge.

Romance and sex.

The desire for honour and morality.

The desire to have and raise children.

Seeking power and influence.

Curiosity and the desire to learn.

The desire to be independent and make our own decisions.

The desire for status and prestige.

The desire for public service and social justice.

The desire for citizenship and sense of community.

Callers added one more desire to the list: **The wish to earn a secure income.** *Which may remind you of a short rhyme that crops up from time to time:*

> Never ask of money spent
> Where the spender thinks it went.
> Nobody was ever meant
> To remember or invent
> What he did with every cent.

Robert Frost's
'The Hardship of Accounting', 1936

The B in **debt** is silent, but not entirely useless. It suggests a sting.

Love may make the world go round, but the engine room of a stable society is powered by . . .

Three Things

Three things to govern:
Temper, tongue, conduct.

Three things to cultivate:
Tolerance, affection, patience.

Three things to commend:
Thrift, industry, punctuality.

Three things to despise:
Cruelty, arrogance, ingratitude.

Three things to admire:
Dignity, courage, loyalty.

Three things to give:
Comfort to the sad, appreciation to the worthy . . . and love.

For all Australians, the most meaningful words spoken anywhere—on TV, radio, at war memorials throughout the nation, in RSL Clubs—are surely . . .

For the Fallen

They shall grow not old, as we that are left grow old:
Age shall not weary them, nor the years condemn.
At the going down of the sun and in the morning
We will remember them.

by Laurence Binyon

The listener who faxed in the following pointed out that he was a severely disabled pensioner. As such, the words held a very special meaning for him.

I Am Most Richly Blessed

I asked for strength that I might achieve greatness.
I was made weak that I might learn humbly to obey.

I asked for health that I might do greater things.
I was given infirmity that I might do better things.

I asked for riches that I might be happy.
I was given poverty that I might be wise.

I asked for power that I might have the praise of men.
I was given weakness that I might feel the need of God.

I asked for all things that I might enjoy life.
I was given life that I might enjoy all things.

I got nothing that I asked for,
    but everything that I hoped for.

Almost despite myself,
    my unspoken prayers were answered.

I am among all men, most richly blessed.

Rabindranath Tagore

The Pick of "Thought for the Day"

- The problem with the genepool is that there's no lifeguard.

- There are times when we all feel like we're diagonally parked in a parallel universe.

- You are as young as your faith and as old as your despair.

- We can't direct the wind, but we can adjust the sails.

- People wrapped up in themselves make a very small package.

116

Talking Time

It's no coincidence that time is known as the Fourth Dimension, and the media is called the Fourth Estate. Radio has always been driven by the tyranny of time, although these days the domination is digital. But for most of us procrastination, the art of keeping up with yesterday, rules. Bernard Berenson once said: 'I wish I could stand on a busy corner, hat in hand, and beg people to throw me all their wasted hours.' In radio, words should be weighed, not counted. In life, time is better counted than weighed. It can prove heavy sometimes.

Timely Facts & Figures

- In an average lifetime you will spend 8 years at work and 4 years eating, 5 years standing and 12 years talking, 2 years unsuccessfully returning phonecalls, 1 year searching for misplaced objects, 9 months opening junk mail and 8 months waiting at traffic lights. And through it all you'll blink 415 million times and your heart will pump over 2,500,000,000 live-preserving beats.

- If you live to 70, you'll have at your disposal about 613,600 hours. 204,400 will be devoted to sleep, 176,800 will be spent at work or school, 51,100 will be used for eating, bathing and going to the toilet, 38,325 will go in travelling from here to there, and 76,000 will be spent on household chores. This leaves you with only 66,975 hours for personal enjoyment. So *stop procrastinating*!

- **What could happen in the next five minutes?** The world's human population will increase by 900. Your lungs could process 40,000 cubic cm of air; while boiling a medium-soft egg you could watch the sun burn 1,200,000,000 tonnes of hydrogen; and you could lose your car (one stolen every five minutes).

Time and the Fashion Countdown

The same dress which is 'indecent' 10 years before its time, is 'daring' 1 year before its time, 'chic' in its time, 'dowdy' 3 years after its time, 'hideous' 20 years after its time, 'amusing' 30 years after its time, 'romantic' 100 years after its time and 'beautiful' 150 years after its time.

UK fashion expert James Laver

Er, hang on a sec . . .

Now that the clocks have been turned back, have you noticed it gets late very early?

And why are the days longer in summer than in winter? Is it because they expand with the heat?

Don't bother doing the arithmetics.
Just enjoy . . .

Why I Won't Give You a Day Off

There are 365 days in the year. You sleep eight hours a day, making 122 days which, subtracted from 365 days, makes 243 days.

You also have eight hours of recreation every day, making another 122 days which, subtracted from 243 days, leaves a balance of 121 days.

There are 52 Sundays you don't work, which leaves 69 days. You also get Saturday afternoons off—52 half days—or 26 more days that you do not work.

You get an hour for each lunch which, when totalled, makes 19 days, leaving 27 days of the year.

You get 21 days holiday each year, so that leaves 6 days. And you take five public holidays during the year, which leaves only one day.

And I'll be damned if I will give you that one day off!

And here's the information many requested on those traditional . . .

Wedding Anniversary Gifts

1st	paper	14th	ivory
2nd	cotton	15th	crystal
3rd	leather	20th	china
4th	silk	25th	silver
5th	wood	30th	pearl
6th	iron	35th	coral
7th	wool	40th	ruby
8th	bronze	45th	sapphire
9th	copper	50th	gold
10th	tin/aluminium	55th	emerald
11th	steel	60th	diamond
12th	linen	65th	blue sapphire
13th	lace	70th	platinum

Radio talkshows don't attract only the over 40s. You know when it's school exam time. The more cunning students call the open line with such appeals as: help! I have six hours to complete a project on . . .

The Origin of the Clock

Devices for recording time have been around since 3500 BC.

First came the primitive stick sundial used by the Babylonians, then water clocks, sand or hour glasses and a form of candle clock.

Mechanical clocks with bells to mark the hours arrived on the scene in the early 1300s AD.

Clocks with hands and faces appeared in the 1400s and, by 1450, a simple spring-driven clock had been invented.

In the 1600s Galileo and Huygens gave us the pendulum clock, and the first electric clocks were telling the time in the 1840s.

Why Time Is Measured in 24 Hours

The sun rises in the east and sets in the west. Early civilisations generally, and those clever Babylonians in particular, naturally fell into the pattern of using daylight most efficiently—dawn, morning, afternoon and evening, with a break for nourishment in the middle of the day. Night was for sleeping and keeping watch.

The four daytime periods were each divided into three segments giving a total of twelve which, for the Babylonians, was a mystical number being divisible by 1, 2, 3, 4 and 6.

With night matching day the 24 hour clock was established. The word 'hour' comes from the Latin 'hora'.

And for the terminally curious, here's . . .

Who Gave February Only Twenty-eight Days?

Thirty days hath September,
April, June and November;
All the rest have thirty-one
Excepting February alone:
Which has but twenty-eight, in fine,
Till leap year gives it twenty-nine.

When he reformed the Roman calendar in 46 BC, Julius Caesar based it on the solar cycle. Previously it had been based on the moon's patterns, but this left every year 11.25 days short and out of sync with the seasons.

Caesar's plan was five months of thirty days, and six months of thirty-one days. One month, February, had twenty-nine with thirty each leap year.

To leave his mark on the new system, Julius renamed Quintillis, the seventh month, after himself: July.

Later, another Roman emperor, Augustus Caesar, also wanted a month to bear his name. The eighth month, Sextillia, was renamed August. But it only had thirty days. Not wanting to be outdone by Julius, he increased it to thirty-one—by stealing a day from February.

sourced from the Sunday Herald Sun
Sunday *magazine*

Time Zones

The introduction of the telegraph and development of major railways in the mid 19th century highlighted the need for a globally recognised system of time zones.

In August 1884 an International Meridian Conference accepted proposals which would see 12 time zones west of Britain's Greenwich Observatory, the 'prime meridian' or 0 degrees longitude, and 12 to the east.

These zones divide the globe into 23 full zones, and two half-zones. The 12th zone east, and the 12th zone west are each half-a-zone wide. They lie next to each other and are separated by an imaginary line called the International Date Line.

also the ticklish question of . . .

Why a Week Has Seven Days

Cambridge University researchers believe the answer may lie in the humble body louse.

Our earliest ancestors could wear their crude clothes fairly comfortably for six days. But biting experience taught them that if they didn't pound out the dirt and bugs in a nearby stream on the seventh day, by day eight the lice had multiplied.

As ritual was used as a tribal glue, the seventh delousing day would have been linked with some deity or rites to make it special. Much later, Genesis in the Old Trestament picked this up and turned it into the day God rested.

If each of us kept just one old-fashioned clock in the home, the ticking of the seconds and chiming of the hours would serve to remind us that time is . . .

The Currency of Life

If you had a bank account that, every morning, credited your account with $86,400, carried over no balance, allowed no cash to remain in the account and, at the end of the day, cancelled what you failed to use—what would you do? Withdraw it fast, correct? Believe it or not, you do have such an account and it is time.

Each morning you are credited with 86,400 seconds to spend as you wish. Whatever is not used is lost. There are no balances to carry over to the next day; no overdrafts. All records are destroyed when the day ends. If you do not use the daily deposit, the loss is all yours. There are no returns, no drawing against tomorrow. **Time: a thousand times more valuable than the coin of the realm.**

Invest and use it wisely.

Take Time

Take time to live:
  it is the price of success.

Take time to think:
  it is the source of power

Take time to read:
  it is the fountain of wisdom.

Take time to be friendly:
  it is the road to happiness.

Take time to dream:
  it is hitching your wagon to a star.

Take time to laugh:
  it is the music of the soul.

Take time to play with children:
  it is the joy of joys.

Take time to love and be loved:
  it is the privilege of the gods.

Politically correct academics at Middlesex University have tried to ban the terms BC (Before Christ) and AD (Anno Domini) as they might offend non-Christian ethnic groups. They were to be replaced with the tongue-trippers BCE (Before Common Era) and CE (Common Era).

Damn! Just when I was getting used to yesterday, along comes today . . .

Half Century Charter

For Those Who Have Reached the Venerable Age of 50

Henceforth I claim the right, whenever and wherever I see fit, to . . .

- Grow old as disgracefully as I please;
- Balance the giving and taking more in my favour;
- Give a damn;
- Delegate or dodge those tasks I dislike;
- Indulge in gluttony and sloth;
- Wear comfortable clothes;
- Never again be motivated by guilt;
- Take risks, remembering beaten paths are for beaten people;
- Shed those responsibilities that can now take care of themselves;
- Seek the company of those I enjoy and be unavailable to bores; and
- Express my views honestly, whether asked to or not.

I also demand the right to . . .

- Give myself toys and time to play with them;
- Be my own best friend;
- Transform old bad habits into new art forms;
- Change my mind; and
- Take no crap.

I promise myself I will . . .

- Stop agonising and start organising;
- Give in to temptation;
- Get around to doing all those things I said I would get around to doing one day;
- Revisit my childhood dreams and start realising them; and
- Bury my regrets.

But, most of all, I will . . .

- Reduce the clutter in the cargo hold of my life to one small case of essentials; and
- Record and play back more happy memories, and fewer videos.

This charter has been signed before two sober witnesses

Day: . . . . . . **Month:** . . . . **Year:** . . . .

S. Marsden

Arguments about the year 2000 will continue to rage on radio well into the new millenium. For instance, on the first day of which year do we officially enter a millennium? And does the year 2000 have significance for everyone?

Solving the Millennium Mystery

- Prof. Paul Davies has settled the most contentious dispute. He says our calendar was devised before the concept of zero was known in Europe, so the first year was called 1 AD. Therefore 2000 years won't be up until December 31st 2000. The new millennium starts on January 1st 2001.

- The Muslim, Jewish and Chinese calendars are not the same as our Gregorian calendar, so the year 2000 has special meaning only for Christians. But even then, history records that King Herod died in 4 BC. So if the New Testament stories are correct, Jesus must have been been born before 4 BC. This means that the two-thousandth anniversary of the first Christmas probably fell somewhere between 1991 and 1996.

Get ready to reset your GPS and fasten your seat belt! Continental Australia is moving north at the speed it takes for a fingernail to grow.

And if you thought the moon was looking a tad smaller than it did in your courting days, you're right. It's drawing away from the earth at the rate of four centimetres each year. That adds up to over thirty metres in an average lifetime.

Verse & Worse

Imposing any sort of correctness on talkback would be like punching holes in the ocean. It can't be done. Which is just as well, or many of the contributions in this section would never have made it to your speakers. In 1998 the site of laughter was discovered in the human brain. Located on the left-hand side of the frontal lobe it's about the size of a walnut. Just thought you ought to know that before you continue . . .

While ROM and RAM are depriving our laptop literate five-year-olds of their REM, a happy compatability between the World Wide Web and trailing-edge-technology wireless has brought us fresh new Treasures like . . .

A Clone Pome

Mary had a little lamb
Its fleece was slightly grey.
It didn't have a father,
Just some borrowed DNA.

It sort of had a mother,
Though the ovum was on loan.
It was not so much a lambkin
As a little lamby clone.

And soon it had a fellow clone,
And soon it had some more.
They followed her to school one day
All cramming through the door.

It made the children laugh and sing,
The children found it droll,
There were far too many lamby clones
For Mary to control.

No other could control the sheep
Since their programs didn't vary,
So the scientists resolved it all
By simply cloning Mary.

But now they feel quite sheepish,
Those scientists unwary.
One problem solved, but what to do
With Mary, Mary, Mary?

When Your Computer Bytes Back
The Best of the Top 50 Geek T-shirt Slogans

- Computers make very fast, very accurate mistakes
- Does fuzzy logic tickle?
- File not found. Should I fake it? (Y/N)
- Access denied—nah nah na nah nah!
- Windows. Just another pane in the glass.
- As a computer, I find your faith in technology amusing.
- Press <CTRL><ALT><DEL> to continue.
- Smash forehead on keyboard to continue.
- Press any key . . . no, no, no **not that one!**
- Why doesn't DOS ever say '**Excellent** command or file name'?
- Bad command. Bad, bad command! Sit! Stay! Stay . . .

There are some perfectly good reasons . . .

Why a Necktop Computer Is Better Than a Laptop

It is self-propelled.

It can be mass-produced by unskilled, unpaid labour.

It is so economical it can be run on the equivalent of a handful of peanuts a day.

Its hard drive has unlimited storage and recall capacity and its colour can be changed to suit your decor.

Best of all, it can smile.

Temperance Tour

Anti-Alcohol League,
Rev. Thomas Jones-White,
The Manse,
Boysen, NSW

Dear _____

Perhaps you have heard of my organisation and my international campaign in the cause of temperance. Each year for the past fourteen years I have conducted tours of Australia, New Zealand and the South Pacific delivering a series of lectures on the evils of consuming alcoholic beverages and associated vices.

On those tours I have been accompanied by my friend and assistant, Clyde Linson. Clyde, a young man once of high ideals and impeccable background became a pathetic example of life ruined by excessive indulgence in smoked substances, whisky and women.

Clyde would appear with me at lectures sitting out front on the platform drunk, sweating profusely, wheezing, belching, breaking wind, staring at ladies lewdly through bloodshot eyes and making obscene gestures. I would point him out as an example of what unbridled debauchery can do to a person.

Unfortunately, Clyde has died and gone to his eternal rest.

A mutual friend of ours has provided me with your name. I wonder if you would be available to take Clyde's place on my next tour. If you are, please contact me at the above address at your earliest convenience.

Yours faithfully,
Rev. Thomas Jones-White

The place for all chain letters, no matter what they threaten, is the garbage bin. Except, perhaps, this one . . .

Ball and Chain Letter

Dear Friend,

This letter was started by a woman like yourself, in the hope of bringing relief to the tired and discontented.

Unlike most chain letters, this one does not cost anything. Just send a copy to five of your female friends who are tired and discontented. Then bundle up your husband or boyfriend and send him to the woman whose name appears at the top of the list.

When your name comes to the top, you will receive 10,260 men, and some of them are bound to be a hell of a lot better than the one you already have.

Do not break the chain. Have faith. One woman broke the chain and got her own husband back.

Yours in expectation,

PS: At the time of writing a friend of mine had already received 150 men. They buried her yesterday. It took three undertakers 36 hours to get the smile off her face.

Composed in 1946 by a British Weapons Technical Staff member at the ministry of Supply, this verse loses none of its appeal when applied to our Australian equivalent.

Civil Servants

We're known as civil servants,
   but we don't really deserve
That misapplied description,
   for we certainly don't serve.
Nor are we even civil,
   but in language plain and crude,
We have no effing manners;
   we're simply effing rude.

We never make decisions—
merely pass the buck again,

For to make our sluggish minds up
is beyond our feeble brain.

Obstruction is our watchword,
and if we should succeed

In wrecking some departments,
well, that's today's good deed.

We're rather curious creatures,
for lots of us are cracked.

And lots are damned incompetent,
but none is ever sacked;

For if we make a mess of things
and get the bloody 'bird',

We're soon promoted in the branch
to which we are transferred.

Beware the Bookworm!

From him that stealth or borroweth and returneth not this book from its owner, let it change into a serpent in his hand and rend him.

Let him be struck with palsy and all his members blasted.

Let him languish in pain crying aloud for mercy, and let there be no surcease to his agony till he sing in dissolution.

Let bookworms gnaw his entrails in token of the worm that dieth not, and when at last he goeth to his final punishment, let the flames of hell consume him forever.

from M. Eberhart's 1991
The Whole Library Handbook

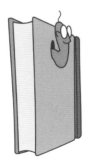

The dumber people are, the more illness and fatigue they have to cope with. People get sick and tired of them. Which brings us to the . . .

Moron's Medical Dictionary

Artery:	the study of painting
Bacteria:	back door of a cafeteria
Barium:	what doctors do when patients die
Bowel:	a letter like a.e.i.o.u.
Caesarian section:	neighbourhood in Rome
Cat scan:	searching for kitty
Cauterise:	made eye contact with her
Coma:	a punctuation mark
Dilate:	to live longer
Enema:	not a friend
Fester:	quicker
Fibula:	a small lie
Genital:	not a jew
Hangnail:	coathook
Impotent:	distinguished, well known
Labour pains:	work-related soreness
Medical staff:	senior doctor's walking stick
Nitrates:	cheaper than day rates
Node:	was aware of
Outpatient:	a person who has fainted
Pap smear:	fatherhood test
Pharmacists:	cattleman's calluses
Recovery room:	upholstery workplace
Rectum:	damn near killed'em
Secretion:	hiding something
Seizure:	Roman emperor
Tablet:	small table
Terminal illness:	sick at airport
Urine:	opposite of 'you're out'
Varicose:	nearby
Vein:	conceited

From an Aussie sportsman competing overseas: 'Mate, this hotel is a dump. The cockroaches are so big they crow at sunrise!'

Mother-in-law jokes, golliwogs, primary school nativity plays, Christmas carols and even Christmas itself (remember Winterval?) have all been picked on by the po-faced PC. Thank goodness the Irish sense of humour endured the purge.

Irish Government Pipe Specifications

1   All pipe is to be made of a long hole surrounded by metal or plastic centred around the hole.

2   All pipe is to be hollow throughout the entire length. Do not use holes of a different length than the pipe.

3   The I.D. (inside diameter) of all pipe must not exceed the O.D. (outside diameter), otherwise the hole will be on the outside.

4   All pipe over 50 feet (15 m) in length should have the words **long pipe** clearly stamped on each end, so the contractor will know it is a long pipe.

5   Pipe over 2 miles (3.2 km) in length must also have the words **long pipe** stamped in the middle, so the contractor will not have to walk the entire length of the pipe to determine its size.

6   All pipe over 6 inches (152 mm) in diameter must have the words **large pipe** stamped on it so the contractor will not mistake it for small pipe.

7   Flanges must be used on all pipes. Flanges must have holes for all bolts quite separate from the big hole in the middle.

8   When ordering 90 degree, 45 degree or 30 degree elbows, be sure to specify right or left hand, otherwise the pipe will go the wrong way.

9   It is essential to specify to your vendor whether you want level, uphill or downhill pipe. If you use a downhill pipe for uphill purposes, the water will not flow as required.

10 All couplings should have either right-hand or left-hand threads, but do not mix the threads, otherwise, as the coupling is being screwed onto one pipe, it will be unscrewed from the other which would result in a leaky joint.

The original Murphy's Law actually saved lives of airmen (see Game of the Name). These later laws created in his name were sent to the studio printed on an Irish linen teatowel:

Murphy's Law: Anything That Can Go Wrong, Will

- Anything good in life is either illegal, immoral or fattening.
- It's morally wrong to allow suckers to keep their money.
- The light at the end of the tunnel is an oncoming train.
- Celibacy is not hereditary.
- Beauty is only skin deep, ugly goes to the bone.
- Never play leapfrog with a unicorn.
- A Smith & Wesson beats four aces.
- If everything seems to be going well, you obviously don't know what the hell is going on.
- Never argue with a fool. People might not know the difference.
- A short cut is the longest distance between two points.
- Friends come and go, but enemies accumulate.
- The other line always moves faster.
- A race is not always to the swift nor the battle to the strong, but that's the way to bet.
- Anything you try to fix yourself will take longer and cost more than you thought.
- The repairman will never have seen a model quite like yours before.
- In order to get a loan, you must first prove you don't need it.
- The chance of a piece of bread falling buttered side down is directly proportional to the cost of the carpet.

Home dressmakers will identify with this lesser-known list of laws snipped from a lifestyle talkshow:

Murphy's 18 Laws of Sewing

1 Fusible interfacings always fuse to the iron.

2 If you need 6 matching buttons, you will find only 5 in your button box.

3 The seam you meant to rip out is invariably the other one.

4 The greater your haste, the smaller the eye of the needle you need to thread.

5 The fabric you forgot to pre-shrink will shrink most.

6 The favourite pattern you wish to use again will have one key piece missing.

7 If you drop anything out of your sewing basket, it will be your box of pins . . . with the lid off.

8 Whenever the construction process is going well, the bobbin thread runs out.

9 The magnitude of the irreparable mistake is in direct proportion to the cost of the fabric.

10 Your lost needle will be found by a member of your family . . . while walking around barefoot.

11 The more fiddly the facing, the more likely it is to be sewn to the wrong side.

12 Collar points fail to match only when you've trimmed all the seams.

13 The iron never scorches the garment until its final pressing.

14 The steam iron only burps rusty water on light silk fabrics.

15 The sewing machine light only burns out on a Sunday morning.

16 No matter how often you correct it, a circular skirt hem will always dip.

17 A gathered thread always breaks in the middle.

18 The scissors cut easiest past the buttonhole.

A gardening show grievance:
'Perennials are the ones that grow like weeds, biennials are the ones that die this year instead of next and hardy annuals are the ones that never come up at all'.

It may date from the days of boom-boom burlesque, but it's still raising a smile.

A Letter from an Irish Mum to Her Son in Australia

1 High Street,
Ballymary.
Today

Dear Son,

Just a few lines to let you know I'm still alive. I'm writing this letter slowly as I remember you can't read fast. You won't know the house when you come home. We've moved.

Your father has a lovely new job with 500 men under him. He cuts the grass at the cemetery.

There's a washing machine in our new house but it isn't working too good. I put fourteen shirts into it, pulled the chain, and I haven't seen the shirts since.

Your sister Coleen had a baby last week. I haven't found out if it's a boy or girl yet so I don't know if you're an Uncle or Auntie.

Your Uncle Dick drowned in a vat of whiskey in Dublin a few days ago. Some of his mates dived in to save him but he fought them off bravely. We cremated his body and it took three days for the fire to go out.

I went to the doctor on Thursday and your father came with me. The doctor put a tube in my mouth and told me not to open it for ten minutes, then your father offered to buy it from him.

It only rained twice last week, the first time for three days, and the second time for four days. On Monday it was so windy the hen laid the same egg four times.

We had a letter from the undertaker. He said if we don't pay the final instalment on your Granny, up she comes.

Your loving Mum

PS: I was going to send you some money, but I already sealed the envelope.

134

(Politician of Your Choice) Is My Shepherd . . .

I shall not want.
He maketh me to lie down in dry pastures,
He leadeth me beside still factories and abandoned farms,
He restoreth my doubts in the Labor/Liberal Party.
Yea though I walk through the valley of the shadow
    of debts, his staff won't comfort me.
He anointeth my wage with tax and inflation, so my
    expenses runneth over my income.
Surely poverty shall follow me all the days of my life,
And I shall dwell in the subsidised house of the
    Government forever.

Five thousand years ago Moses said,
Pick up your shovel,
Feed your camel,
Move your ass,
And I shall lead you to the promised land.

Five thousand years later Gough Whitlam said,
Lay down your shovel,
Get off your camel,
Sit on your ass,
This is the promised land.

But this year (pollie of choice) will,
Take your shovel,
Sell your camel,
Kick your ass,
And tell you he's sold the promised land.

I'm glad I'm an Aussie.
I'm glad I'm free.
I wish I was a dog and (pollie of choice) was a tree.

When caller and presenter are going at it hammer and tongue, statistics often fly like flak. And you know what they say about statistics . . .. This cock-eyed calculation first appeared in the UK Evening Standard newspaper shortly after WWII. It's been much adapted for local consumption since; here's a recent Australian effort:

It's Time We Faced Up to Our Responsibilities

Population of Australia	18,850,000
People aged 65 or over	7,410,426
Balance left to do the work	11,439,574
People aged under 18	6,722,961
Balance left to do the work	4,716,613
People working for the government	2,628,202
Balance left to do the work	2,088,411
People in the armed forces	503,147
Balance left to do the work	1,585,264
People in nationalised industries	624,629
Balance left to do the work	960,635
People in hospitals and asylums	232,423
Balance left to do the work	728,212
Moonlighters and dole bludgers	716,739
Balance left to do the work	11,473
People in gaol	11,471
Balance left to do the work	**2**

That's two people left, you and me; so you'd better pull your finger out and get to work, because **I'm sick of running this country by myself!**

ABC radio announcer:
'Don't worry if you're not listening now, as the program will be repeated on Monday Evening.'

Radio's Most Tasteless (and Tasty?) News Item

British law frowns on the killing and maiming of fellow humans but, as was pointed out in Parliament in January 1998, *eating* body parts is still allowed.

Which brings us to . . .

The Human Placenta Pâté Party

In February 1998, Channel 4 TV viewers in England were treated to the screening of an unusual cooking program. With camera crew at the ready, a culinary triumph made from the frozen afterbirth of baby Indie-Mo was served on homemade focaccia bread and presented to 20 guests at her *Welcome to the World* celebration. And yes, when the story broke on Australian radio, listeners cheerfully sent in their stamped self-addressed envelopes for the recipe. So, in case you missed it . . .

How to Make Human Placenta Pâté

Ingredients:

1 placenta	1 tablespoon sage
2 shallots	and parsley, chopped
2 garlic cloves	brandy to flambé
60g softened butter	½ lime, squeezed
olive oil for frying	salt and pepper to taste

Method:

1 Prepare placenta by running under cold water for a few minutes to remove blood. Take off tough outer membrane. Chop into small chunks.

2 Heat oil in pan. Add shallots and garlic, then placenta chunks. Fry until brown.

3 When nearly cooked, flambé with the brandy, then remove from heat.

4 Put half the mixture into a food processor with the softened butter and chopped herbs, and blend.

5 Chop the remaining portion very finely and add to the blended mixture. Add the lime juice, season to taste and serve on crackers or buttered toast.

To follow that 'entrée' try this
GAS-tronomic treat . . .

Roast Duck Stromboli

Ingredients:

1 duck	4 slices pineapple
3 eggs	500g dry uncooked popcorn

Method:

1 Mix dry ingredients, add eggs and pineapple.

2 Place duck in oven (350°F) and cook for one hour.

3 Remove duck from oven. Stuff with mixed ingredients and replace in oven.

4 Cooking should be completed when the popcorn blows the arse out of the duck.

Using a map and imagination, this 70-year-old survivor of the London vaudeville stage can be adapted to just about any city or community. What's more, it's withstood the talkback test of time without any obvious divine retribution. To enjoy the full impact it should be read aloud.

The Lord's Prayer: S.A. Version

Our Father who art in **Hendon**,
Hallet Cove be thy **Glynde**. Thy **Croydon** come,
Thy **Kensington** in **Firle**, as it is in **Hackham**.
Give us **Largs Bay** our daily **Grange**
And forgive us our **Thebarton**, as we forgive them
That **Tranmere** against us.
Lead us not into **South Plympton**,
But deliver us from **Enfield**.
For Thine is the **Kingston**, the **Para** and the **Gawler**,
For **Exeter** and **Ethelton**,
Mile End.

(For non-Adelaideans, Thebarton is pron: **Theb**-*er-ton)*

13 Call Coaxers

When the evening switchboard falls silent, all the commercials have been aired, all the songs on the log have been played and the cleaner has walked off with the only newspaper in the studio, what's urgently required is a Call Coaxer—something that motivates listeners to lift the receiver and dial the magic number.

First rule of talk broadcasting: let the listeners do the work. An audience can become lazy if served a steady diet of editorial comment. What people need is food for thought and the prospect of a prize. Ask, for instance, for the wittiest contributions to . . .

People to Avoid at Parties

The bloke in the 1996 Formula 1 Grand Prix jacket.

The person who's actually read *Satanic Verses*.

People who still have a red nose on their car.

The woman wearing dolphin earrings, bible sandals and tie-dye skirt who asks what star sign you are.

The suit with an obvious hair transplant, a mobile phone on one hip and pager on the other.

The born-again Christian you wished hadn't been born in the first place.

or how about . . .

If Genetic Engineers are So Smart Why Don't They . . .

- design a spray we can squirt into the atmosphere to reconstruct the ozone layer.
- switch on the honesty gene in politicians.
- develop woolly babies who moult at about three when they learn to dress themselves.
- create anti-cancer caulis, sprouts and cabbages that smell and taste of hot, salty chips.

- fine-tune the male memory so females will never again hear cries of 'darl, where's the . . . ?' or worse, 'where the hell have you put my . . . ?
- eradicate the guilt gene in women.
- work on a credibility gene for journalists?

and then there are . . .

The Most Unpleasant Sounding Words in the English Language

(top ten according to the US National Assoc. of Speech)

- phlegmatic;
- gripe;
- plump;
- flatulent;
- sap;
- jazz;
- plutocrat;
- cacophony;
- crunch; and
- treachery.

If the 'Silence of the Cans' situation continues, this hoary old riddle should liven things up: (Danger! Marriages have been destroyed over less . . . oh, and cans are headphones).

A man is looking at a photograph. He says: 'Brothers and sisters have I none, but this man's father is my father's son.' Who is he looking at?
Answer: His son.

Disbelievers, work it backwards . . . we'll call the man looking at the photograph Kevin. Kevin says, the **father** of the person in the photo ('this man's father') is the son of Kevin's father ('is my father's son'). Kevin is the son of Kevin's father, so Kevin is the father of the person in the photo.

Did You Know . . .

- that Tonga once produced a postage stamp in the shape of a banana?
- that the words 'abstemious' and 'facetious' both contain all the vowels in order?
- that if your career choice is being a ceremonial footman at Buckingham Palace, you must have a chest measurement of exactly 96 centimetres?
- that HAL, the bossy computer in the movie *2001: A Space Odyssey*, was named by taking the three letters in the alphabet which precede IBM?
- that Australian author Patrick White said his mother's mouth was always set at twenty past seven?
- that the first aeroplane fitted with a lavatory was the Russian passenger transport Russky Vitiaz in 1913?
- that if you put a kitten into a room with only horizontal stripes, when freed 6 months later it would not be able to climb anything vertical?
- that a Boeing 777 has 3 million parts, weighs 540,000 kilos and would take 20 years to get to the sun?
- that the top speed of a dragonfly is 98.6 km/h?
- that a snail's pace is exactly 0.05 km/h?
- that onions are never on the menu in a submarine?

They've got whiskers on, but they're still fun . . .

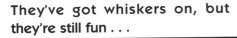

Batty Book Titles

The Insomniac by Eliza Wake

The Tiger's Revenge by Claude Body

Drunk and Disorderly by Honor Bender

The Postscript by Adeline Ecstra

The Barber of Seville by Ray Zerr

Influenza by Mike Robe

My Most Embarrassing Moment by Lucy Lastick

One exercise that will turn on lexiphiles among the listeners is working out . . .

Palindromes

(words or sentences that read the same forwards and backwards)

EVIL I DID DWELL; LEWD DID I LIVE

MADAM, I'M ADAM

WAS IT A CAR OR A CAT I SAW?

ABLE WAS I ERE I SAW ELBA

A MAN, A PLAN, A CANAL—PANAMA

SUMS ARE NOT SET AS A TEST ON ERASMUS

I MAN AM REGAL. A GERMAN AM I

RISE TO VOTE, SIR

Here are a few colourful collective terms for animals. Why not invent some for human groups? A ransom of plumbers, a clique of photographers . . .

A shrewdness of apes

A clowder of cats

A murder of crows

A skulk of foxes

A balding (on land), paddling (on water), of ducks

A cast of hawks

An ostentation of peacocks

A smack of jellyfish

Second rule of talk broadcasting:
Keep listeners busy. This is where
puzzles and riddles come in useful.
Some of these have been around
even longer than radio . . .

Make 1000 by using only 8s.
Answer: 8+8+8+88+888

Three women had two daughters each and they all went out for a meal in a restaurant. A waiter looked at the group and said 'A table for seven, ladies?' Why seven?
Answer: One of the women is the grandmother.

Write down your age, double it, add 5, multiply by 50, subtract 365, add the number of coins in your pocket or purse. Add 115.
Answer: The first two figures will give your age, the last two the number of coins.

Three men book into a motel and pay $10 each for a $30 room. Too late, the receptionist remembers there's a $25 special on rooms today, so she gives the bellboy $5 to return to the three men. As it doesn't divide, he pockets $2 and hands them $1 each. So each man has now paid $9 for the room, which equals $27 total. Add on the $2 in the bellboy's pocket and that give's you $29.
Where's the other dollar?

Write down how many days a week you'd like to have off, multiply by 2, add 5, multiply the total by 50. Add 1,748 if you've had your birthday this year. Add 1,747 if you have not had your birthday this year. Subtract your birth year.
Answer: You should now have the number you started with followed by your age.

A man was locked in a windowless cell with just a table. How did he get out? (a children's riddle from the Victorian era still going strong)
Answer: He rubbed his hand on the wall until it was sore (saw). He sawed the table in half. Two halves make a whole (hole) so he crawled to freedom through the hole.

And a sneaky way to discover someone's age if they're reluctant to reveal it: Ask your victim to think of a number, double it, add their age, halve the total, and take away the number they first thought of.
Answer: The person's age is double what they are left with.

Write down a number between 1 and 9, multiply it by 9, add the numbers in the total together, take away 5. Translate the result into a letter of the alphabet (A=1, B=2 etc.). Pick a country starting with that letter. Take the second letter in that country's name and choose an animal starting with that letter. Write down the colour of that animal.
Answer: Ninety percent have written 'a grey elephant from Denmark'.

G.B Shaw proved that GHOTI spells FISH (cough, women, station). But what does GHOUGHBTEIGHPTEAU spell?

Answer:		
GH as in HICCOUGH	P
OUGH as in DOUGH	O
BT as in DEBT	T
EIGH as in NEIGHBOUR	A
PT as in PTARMIGAN	T
EAU as in BEAU	O

Name a 7-letter word with no vowels.
Answer: rhythms

Anagrams can become addictive, and surprisingly descriptive:

Hated for ill	Adolf Hitler
A decimal point	A dot in place
One hug	Enough?
The eyes	They see
The Mona Lisa	No hat, a smile
The nudist colony	No untidy clothes
Flit on, cheering angel	Florence Nightingale
The warm lion *or* woman Hitler	Mother-in-law

Recent research reveals that little of the brain is a wasteland; most of it is in use all of the time and each portion has its purpose, even if it's only a back-up. You can give your brains a workout, achieve immortality and fill otherwise unoccupied airwaves by creating a new word for the next generation. Here are ten to get you going.

Neology for the New Millennium

Porndromat: internet censor service.

Gerrymanna: spiritual nourishment derived from a political advantage.

Hunkydormant: what stressed-out Chippendales and Manpower performers can become.

Constipedia: condition afflicting former joggers.

Dicoterie: people who still remember exactly what they were doing when the death was announced of Diana, the Princess of Wales.

Aloevehement: maintaining trust, regardless, in natural remedies.

Indigenal: (genal: pertaining to the cheek) describes white people falsely claiming aboriginality for personal gain.

Buyass: shopaholic tendency.

Cobber barons: those who indulge in corporate cronyism.

P-scenery: personalised clutter users place on and around their computer monitors.

Some people hold great store by their job title. The more important it sounds, the better they feel about themselves. Which gives us yet another opportunity for call coaxing fun:

Lofty Names for Humble Occupations

Media Distribution Operative—Delivers Newspapers

Gostopologist—Works the Stop/Go Signs at Roadworks

Suctional Engineer—Carpet Cleaner

Transportation Expeditor—Taxi Driver

Information Choreographer—Librarian

Waste Disposal Operative—Garbage Collector

Destination Counsellor—Travel Agent

Environmental Hygiene Technician—Cleaner

Independent Management Consultant—Unemployed

Myth Busters

Another function of talkback is settling bets. Picture this: the menfolk are home from the pub, on the Sobriety Scale somewhere between tiddly and totally plastered. They may not remember their names, where they are or much about the past few hours. But they clearly recall who won some weird wager. Presenters cultivating a caring image insist that ten percent of the winnings must be contributed to charity. It is, of course, a hollow gesture.

With instant access to the Internet, experts and well-informed listeners, radio is the ideal referee for barroom bets, however bizarre. Which is how this intriguing collection of myth busters made it into the 'Talkback Trash & Treasure' file.

Myth: Middle Age May Bring a Mid-life Crisis

The good news is, there's no such thing as mid-life crisis. Dr Joseph Tally, Clinical Professor of Family Practise at the University of North Carolina and author of *The Family Practitioners' Guide To Treating Depressive Illnesses*, condemns it as a meaningless cliché.

He says, 'From the day we're born to the day we die we face a series of crises, and they don't become worse or more significant just because we reach the age of 45.' He adds, 'The mid-life crisis has become a convenient excuse for failure at work or in relationships, and for aberrant behaviour either in marriage or business. It has never been defined as a clinical syndrome.'

Myth: Wear White to Stay Cool

Black loose clothes are cooler in hot weather than white loose clothes. Black draws hot air more than twice as fast as white creating a chimney effect that accelerates the evaporation of sweat. So those tent-clad ladies in the more strict Islamic nations have got it right.

Myth: SOS Stands for 'Save Our Souls'

The magnetic telegraph was invented in the 1840s by American Samuel Morse. He then went on to create the famous morse code which converted letters and numbers into short and long sound signals.

In 1906 SOS replaced the original international wireless telegraphy 'all ships' distress signal CQD. Members of the Berlin Radio Telegraphic Convention decided its **dot dot dot—dash dash dash—dot dot dot** was a simpler message to transmit and recognise. Only later did popular use turn it into an acronym for Save Our Souls. That other distress call **mayday** comes from the French word m'aidez, assist me.

Myth: You Are 100 Percent Human

According to a report in the *British Medical Journal* quoted by Dr Adam Taor in the May 15th 1998 issue of *Australian Doctor*, adults are made up of one-hundred-million-million cells, but only ten percent of them are human. The rest belong to bacteria, fungi, protozoa, worms and even insects living inside and on us. Hence the current concern over the use of antibiotics.

Myth: Antidisestablishmentarianism Is Our Longest Word

The safest English language expert to trust on this particular chestnut is Giles Brandreth, author of *The Word Book* (Robson Books UK). He says that the longest word in the Oxford English Dictionary is:

floccinaucinihilipilification (29 letters).

It means 'the action or habit of esteeming as worthless' and was first recorded in 1741. Poet Willam Shenstone and Sir Walter Scott both used it.

For wager purposes perhaps we should eliminate any nonsense words or scientific terms such as the protein with a name consisting of 1,913 letters noted in the *Guinness Book of Records*.

But there is a 45-letter name for a lung disease found among miners listed in Webster's *Third International Dictionary* (1961):

pneumonoultramicroscopicsilicovolcanoconiosis.

The winner? Possibly the 37-word adverb used in Mark McShane's 1963 novel *Untimely Ripped*:

praetertranssubstantiationalistically.

Myth: Pet Owners Enjoy Better Health

A survey reported in the *Medical Journal of Australia* in April 1997 cast serious doubt on this widely held theory. The people *without* pets in the study did not have worse mental or physical health than the pet owners.

Those with pets made 8.9 GP visits and 2.5 specialist visits a year, compared with those without pets who made 8.7 and 2.7 visits respectively.

Where the original *National People and Pets* survey may have got it wrong is in the way the figures were obtained. Dr Andrew Jorm of the ANU Psychiatric Epidemiology Research Centre suggests they relied on patient recall rather than Medicare data, and had a selection bias with younger, fitter people.

Myth: Freudian Slips Reveal Hidden Meanings

According to James Reason, a research psychologist at the University of Manchester, a Freudian slip indicates no significant motives or meanings. He says it's just a normal slip of the tongue. A more familiar or simpler word replaces the intended one because of a failure in mental editing.

Myth: The Stars and Stripes Is an All-American Flag

The star-spangled banner Americans fly with such pride was created from the British ancestral family coat-of-arms of George Washington which can still be seen today at Washington Hall in Sunderland, in the north-east of England. The coat-of-arms consists of stars across the top, with red and white stripes beneath them.

Myth: Hagar Was Horny

Vikings never wore horns on their helmets. They would have snagged on weapons. But the Scandanavian Viking raiders and traders who swept through Europe so effectively from the 8th to the

11th centuries AD were pagans, so leaders of the Christian church at the time had to demonise them. Hence they depicted them at every opportunity with horns—which backfired. Its boost to their image as warriors has lasted for well over a millennium.

Myth: The Bard Wrote 'Gilding the Lily'

It's close, but not close enough. The correct line is 'to paint the lily'. The verse concerned comes from Shakespeare's *King John*, Act IV, scene ii. It reads:

To gild refined gold, to paint the lily,
To throw a perfume on the violet,
To smooth the ice or add another hue
Unto the rainbow, or with a taper-light
To seek the beauteous eye of heaven to garnish,
Is wasteful and ridiculous excess.

Myth: Fright Can Turn Your Hair White Overnight

Despite apocryphal stories to the contrary, hair that is already brown, black, blonde or any colour other than grey and white cannot lose its colour spontaneously.

But it is possible for severe stress to cause those tougher coloured hairs to fall out over a period of days, leaving behind on the scalp finer white and grey hairs. This may give the impression that the victim has 'turned white overnight'.

Also, failure of the colouring mechanism at the root of each hair can occur suddenly following serious illness or shock. Even then, only new hairs growing through at the normal rate would appear white or light grey.

Myth: Posh Means Port-Out-Starboard-Home

In nineteenth century Romany slang, **posh** meant 'a dandy' or 'money'. According to Nigel Rees' *Dictionary of Word and Phrase Origins* (Cassell), the P&O liner-related meaning suggesting that the priciest staterooms were on the shady side of the ship to and from the United Kingdom and British India, is probably incorrect. There was no cost difference between first class port or starboard cabins and, anyway, the discomfort in the hot weather would have been the same no matter on which side they were located.

Myth: Cricket's Top Trophy Contains a Burnt Bail

It's now believed the tiny urn that sits permanently at the Marylebone Cricket Club, along with its red and gold velvet bag and a scorecard from an 1882 Test match between Australia and England, probably contains the ashes of a lady's veil, not a bail.

To mourn England's defeat at the The Oval on August 20th, a journalist penned an obituary for English cricket which concluded 'The body will be cremated and the Ashes taken to Australia'. A few weeks later in Victoria, Australia was beaten by an English team led by Ivo Bligh, Lord Darnley.

Following the victory a group of Melbourne women, including Florence Rose Murphy, the future Lady Darnley, presented Bligh with a small urn containing the ashes of what he understood to be a burnt bail. But well over a hundred years later family members have suggested it is the remains of Florence's veil in the urn. She had worn and then burnt it while Bligh was helping defeat the Aussies.

Myth: Ned's Last Words Were 'Such Is Life'

There are those who firmly believe that Ned Kelly robbed the rich to give to the poor, and that his last words on the gallows were 'Such is life'. Are they merely mythmakers?

Emeritus Professor of Law, historian and author Alex Castles says yes, because they're wrong on both counts. He insists Kelly's last words were probably inaudible to anyone except his hangman Elijah Upjohn who failed to pass them on.

Journalists present at the time were kept well back from the action, and official witnesses who were a little closer believed they heard only 'Ah, well, I suppose . . .' However, even this is in doubt.

Myth: They Let It All Hang Out at Woodstock

In fact, the famous hippy festival wasn't held at Woodstock. It took place some distance away on farmland adjoining the town of Bethel.

Myth: One Day Walt Will Be Defrosted

Rumour has it that before Walt Disney, the father of *Fantasia*, died in 1966 he resorted to cryonics as a means of restoring his mortal coil. But the truth is his remains are resting peacefully in the Disney family tomb.

And in case you ever wondered:

. . . a glow-worm is a beetle, Bombay duck is dried fish, great Danes originated in Germany, lead pencils contain graphite, chop suey is an American invention, a silkworm is a caterpillar, a shooting star is a meteor and sweetbread is the pancreas or thymus gland of an animal.

Notes for Adjudicators:

- Word experts offer seven credible origins of such hotly-debated expressions as 'OK' and 'mind your Ps and Qs', and six of 'pommie'. NB: Variations of that other favourite 'mad as a hatter' were in use long before the unfortunate hat-makers in Lewis Carroll's day were rendered clinically peculiar by the nitrate of mercury used to treat felt (the Anglo Saxon word 'atter' meant poison causing fever).

- It might be worth reminding romantics that the 'I do' component of the marriage vows is a modern American creation perpetuated by TV soaps. It should be 'I will', following the quaint *Book of Common Prayer* question 'Wilt thou have this woman to thy wedded wife?'

- **Misquotes from the movies:** To put the record straight (for those who care about such things), the words 'Beam me up, Scotty' were never spoken in the original *Star Trek* series, Sherlock Holmes never said 'Elementary, my dear Watson' and Humphrey Bogart never uttered the line, 'Play it again, Sam' in the film *Casablanca*.

15 April Fool

How journos love the morning of April 1st. It's where news meets nonsense. But why? There's some disagreement, but our infomedia settled on the fact that All Fools' Day dates from the 1560s when France adopted a reformed calendar which moved New Year's Day from March 25th to January 1st.

Until then, when March 25th fell in Holy Week, the giving of New Year's gifts was postponed until April 1st. For a while pranksters continued to suck in the unsuspecting by visiting and setting up practical jokes. The custom caught on and, surprisingly, survives in one form or another in much of the developed world.

Most zoo staff dread April Fool's Day . . .

Their lines run hot with requests to speak to Mr Lyon, Ellie Fant and Mr G. Raff. Although all news stories broadcast on the first are regarded as suspect, some that later prove to be pranks have a disturbing ring of possibility.

Optometrist-designed prescription windscreens for drivers will be available through state motoring organisations by the end of the year.

Concerned scientists at the NSW Electronic Research Laboratories are advising TV viewers to hang a metal coat-hanger or rod next to the nearest doorway each time they use the remote control. This is to trap hazardous electrons sent ricocheting around the room when they fail to aim straight with the beam.

A corporate sponsorship scheme to be introduced next month by the Federal Education Minister will assist students unable to pay their annual school fees to cover their costs by wearing a firm's logo on uniform blazers, shirts and sportswear.

And from the Wires:

An Adelaide firm has reaped the rewards of 12 years' research by producing its first batch of striped paint. The firm, Lirrap Paints, is releasing the striped paint in the colours of the Adelaide Crows and Port Power in hardware stores this week. The breakthrough came when Loof Lirpa developed a special anti-static clumping effect which improves the surface tension of the paint.

The Weekly Times Messenger

A Japanese recording company's April Fools' joke, a remedy for insomniacs, has turned into an unexpected bestseller. The eighty-five minute cassette recording of a monotonous voice counting sheep proved so popular and apparently effective, a reissue was rushed out within a week. (True!)

United Press International

Would you have believed these?

'A news item just in . . .'

Pumping ions now creating energy: A Tasmanian fitness gym is planning to convert its treadmills, exercise bikes and climbing machines into dynamos that can generate electricity. Management has been advised that, if all suitable equipment could be in full operation for a minimum of 5 hours a day, enough power should be generated to serve all the gym's needs, leaving a significant amount of excess electricity to sell to the Tasmanian grid.

'And from our science and technology correspondent . . .'

Cook books can make you fat: If you're on a diet, steer clear of glossy coffee table cook books! Researchers at Cumbria University's Department of Neuro-psychology have revealed that feasting your eyes on colour photos of high calorie foods can lead to chubbier hips and thighs.

The same power of suggestion that can turn someone consuming a non-alcoholic gin-flavoured soft drink into a rolling drunk, may also trick the brain into believing a colour page spread of a roast dinner is a reality.

You think you are savouring the aroma and taste only in your *imagination*. But to your salivary glands and the neuro-transmitters in your brain, the meal can briefly become very real, causing fat already in your system to be deposited in the energy storage areas of your body in anticipation of more nourishment. Once established, that excess flesh is difficult to shift.

More Newsroom Nonsense

- It was anounced that, to satisfy overseas tourists' expectations, kangaroos would be released in Sydney's Central Business District.

- **A notice appeared in *The Advertiser* stating a 50 km strip of land on the South Australian side of the SA/VIC border would be sold to Victoria for a one-off payment of $8.2 billion.**

- A white coffee bean had been developed for those who do not enjoy black coffee.

- *The Financial Review* **featured a section apparently edited by the alleged corporate outlaw Christopher Skase.**

- A Sydney radio station alerted listeners to a spectacular stunt: a jumbo jet would fly under the harbour bridge.

- **It was revealed Bill Gates' Microsoft empire had made a bid for the Catholic Church.**

- The latest personal computers offered a new motivational facility; they would emit fragrances.

- **Tuna tossing would become an Olympic demonstration sport.**

- A real estate firm had secured The Lodge in Canberra and would be converting it into a boutique hotel.

- **S.A.'s Deputy Premier informed a TV current affairs show audience the State would adopt the 10 hour decimal clock.**

- Anglers were excited to see demonstrated on TV a fishing rod that allowed the user to dial up the type of fish he or she wanted to catch.

- **In the UK, a press report leaked the news that the queen was undergoing DNA testing because a West Country farmer claimed to be the rightful heir to the throne.**

- Stonehenge had been sold to the Japanese to be relocated to Mt Fuji.

- **Virgin chief, Richard Branson, disguised a hot air balloon as a flying saucer creating mayhem in the English countryside.**

- The supposed head of Renault, one Avril Poisson *(Fr: April Fish)* unveiled the world's first flying car.

- **Plans of a bridge linking Tasmania with the mainland had been approved and construction would commence.**

- A pill would soon be available that enabled drunks to become instantly sober.

- **Nessie had left a monster footprint beside the lake.**

some suggested by Rex Jory's column in The Advertiser

And from the International Wires:

WALES April 1: A news item reported on Radio Cardiff this morning has triggered a minor gold rush.

It revealed that free-range chickens reared in a mid-Wales valley are producing eggshells with a measurable gold content.

This is not surprising as, traditionally, wedding rings worn by British monarchs are made of Welsh gold mined in the region.

The highest readings are coming from shells of chickens raised on runs sited in the valley's alluvial areas close to streams.

A creative consultant from London advertising agency Sadim & Sadim will be meeting with local poultry farmers tomorrow to explore niche marketing opportunities.

16 The Game of the Name

Names: always a fertile subject for open line discussion. What you call your child, pet, house, business, car or sports team not only speaks volumes about you, but it can affect the perceptions of others. So when playing the game of the name, what has the radio revealed?

First, some facts about names:

- People with unusual first names often do better in life than people with more common names.

  Reasons:
  1. From early childhood every introduction produces an interested response that stimulates comment or question, which is good for self-acknowledgement.
  2. Mildly exotic names are remembered and enjoyed by those who hear them for the first time.
  3. In formative years, extra personality is required to live up to an unusual name.
  Warning: Outrageous names, or those linked with pop and soap opera personalities can hinder progress, trigger defence mechanisms and reveal the unfortunate owner's age.

- **First impressions:** men called by strong names such as Ben, Bill and John initially are taken seriously. On the other hand, nicknames like Benny, Billy or Johnnie can actually disempower an adult male. Likewise, people might assume a woman called Rose, Rebecca or Susan would be intellectually mature. But a Rosie, Becky or Susie could be regarded as more frivolous.

- **Popular names** in 1997/98 shared by boys and girls were: Jordan, Ashleigh, Brodie, Taylor (Tayla), Chandler, Charlie and Paris.

- **Most unusual girls' names** registered in Australia in the past decade were: sisters Destiny and Harmony, Phoenix, Gypsy, Rebel, Pagan, Heaven-Leigh, Liberty, Blythe, Bliss, Paign, Cinnamon, Pepper, Saffron, Sage, Ginger, Thyme, Misty, Raini, Storm, Rainbow, Sundhine, Auburn, Magenta, Paisley, Velvet, Persia, Jamaica, Montana, Tennessee, Dakota, Indiana, Pandora, Hebe, Aphrodite, Electra, Hero,

Cleopatra, Boadicea, Jezabel, Walburga, Coco, Sade, Delta, Porsche, and Tuppence.

- **Most unusual boys' names** were: Maverick, Ace, Jet, Bond, Blade, Slade, Steed, Bro, Buddy, Buick, Chevy, Freedom, Ulysses, Pericles, Sidhartha, Merlin, Eros, Faust, Lenin, Lennon, Elvis, Jimeoin, Keanu, Macauley, Jarman, Rehn, Chubby, Bligh, Mungo, Zenneth, Mo, Trek, Denver, Texas, Bright, Street, and three brothers Banjo, Dusty and Clancy.

Most Popular Pet Names

- Of the approximately 3 million Australian domestic cats, the top 10 names are: Cat, Puss or Pussy, Smokey, Tiger, Sooty, Tom, No Name, Fluffy, Ginger and Sam.

- The 10 most popular names given to Australia's nearly 4 million pet dogs are, for males: Max, Sam, Jack, Jake, Toby, Charlie, Oscar, Zac, Tyson and Jess; and for females: Jessie, Molly, Chloe, Bonnie, Lucy, Sasha, Sally, Tess, Daisy and Zoe.

- Most unusual names for dogs in 1998 were: Cookie Monster, Death Breath, Fender Bender, Iggy Pup, Kosta Lot, Migraine, Stinkerbelle, Fleabag, Double-O-Seven, and Seiko (watchdog).

(dog data from Dog's Life *magazine)*

With road rage a burgeoning problem, what you carry on your vehicle's number plate can affect your wellbeing.

I Name this Car . . .

- 6ULDV8 *(sexual deviate)*
- CME2C *(see me to see—optician)*
- HUP234 *(gym instructor?)*
- FOOTDR *(podiatrist)*
- 4MYEGO *(on a sporty number)*
- TRUBLU
- URAQT2 *(you are a cutie, too)*
- TAT2ED *(tatooed)*
- BITCH
- MUSCLE

Longest Name?

In January 1997 a New Zealand baby boy was registered as: Anaru Tipene Hamuera Erimana Ngapuhi Maungaturoto Omapere Patutou Kotahitanga Ngatokimatawhaorua Titirangi Ngati-Kahungunu Waikato Ngati-Porou Tainui Morgan.

Some Australian postcoded place names conjour up intriguing images unless, of course, you live there:

Rosebud, Coffin Bay, Hat Head, Eden, Cargo, Nile, Donnybrook, Iron Knob, Geranium, Dark Corner, Gunpowder, Alligator Creek, Comet, Rainbow, Hiawatha, Fairy Dell, Come-By-Chance, Bonnie Doon, Kentucky, Peel, Taylors Arm, Bingo, Thumb Creek, The Risk, Broken Head, Collector and Paradise.

In case you ever wondered who the Robert was in . . .

Bob's Your Uncle

He was Robert Arthur Talbot Gascoyne Cecil, better known as Marquess of Salisbury, the British Prime Minister in 1885.

When relatively unknown Member of Parliament Arthur Balfour was appointed as his Chief Secretary for Ireland, it was noted that the Prime Minister was his Uncle Bob and nepotism was suspected. Hence 'Bob's your uncle' means 'And there you are. It's as simple as that!'

A Rose by any other Name Wouldn't...

- An American survey of businesswomen's names revealed a **corporate prejudice** against sexy names such as Jennifer, Cheryl, Samantha and Dawn, but Alma, Doris, Jane and Mildred would be considered executive material.

- In 1998, British insurance firm Touchline reported that the **safest drivers** were called Ronald, Kenneth, Patricia and Susan. Eight out of ten of the **most accident prone** names were male, the top three being Jason, Darren and Lee. Females who seriously let the side down were Deborah and Clair.

In the early 1900s psychiatrist Carl Jung referred to it as 'the compulsion of the name'. These days it's called 'nominative determinism'. If your name matches your occupation you are not alone; and research suggests it may not be a simple coincidence . . .

The 'Cheat & Prosper, Solicitors' Syndrome

- Membership of the Veterinary Association includes two Dr Birds, two Dr Bullocks, a dog show judge named B. Woof, a Lamb and a Fox, a Sparrow, a Chicken, an Eagle, and a Herring.

- In the world of horse racing, as well as a Ms Horsfall, you'll find a Chris Trott and a Tony Cantor.

- Messrs Vice, Lust and Lusty (*a policeman*) are all involved in explaining or solving problems related to sex.

- And Meteorological Offices around the English speaking world are teeming with people called Rainbow, Rainbird, Storm, Flood, Frost, Weatherall and even Thundercliffe.

Acronyms

Some acronyms are useful. They suggest the function of a group or organisation as in CEASE: Citizens to End Animal Suffering and Exploitation. But two unofficial medical acronyms you don't want to see on that progress chart at the foot of your hospital bed are . . .

FUBAR BUNDY: F . . . ed Up Beyond All Recognition But Unbelievably Not Dead Yet

and . . .

PAFO: Pissed And Fell Over.

Who Was Murphy?

Murphy's Law, also known as Sod's Law, that states 'if anything can go wrong it will go wrong' (see *Verse & Worse*) probably dates back to 1949.

George Nichols, a project manager with Californian aviation firm Northrop, based the law on a sensible suggestion made to him by Capt. E. Murphy of the Wright Field-Aircraft Laboratory. It was applied to avoid aircraft design mistakes, not excuse them.

Lurking among the Wit and Wisdom you'll find the downright Wierd. And they don't come any more eerie than . . .

The Lincoln-Kennedy Coincidence

President Lincoln was elected in 1860.
President Kennedy was elected in 1960.

Both were concerned with Civil rights.
And both lost children while in the White House.

Both men were shot in the head on a Friday in the presence of their wives.
Both were replaced with Southern Democrat Senators named Johnson.

Lincoln's successor, Andrew Johnson was born in 1808.
Kennedy's successor, Lyndon Johnson, was born in 1908.

Booth, Lincoln's murderer, was born in 1839.
Oswald, Kennedy's murderer, was born in 1939.

Both assassins were themselves assassinated before their trials.

Lincoln's secretary was named Kennedy.
Kennedy's secretary was named Lincoln.

Secretary Lincoln advised Kennedy not to go to Dallas.
Secretary Kennedy advised Lincoln not to go to the theatre.

Booth shot Lincoln in a theatre and ran to a warehouse.
Oswald shot Kennedy from a warehouse and ran to a theatre.

From the Wires:

In the United States, an Internet domain name, www.computer.com, has sold for a record US$763,950 (A$ 1.15 million). Former Silicon Valley programmer Kevin Sinclair registered the name and the toll-free telephone number 1 800 COMPUTE in 1994 because he thought "it was cool".

A recent survey reveals that 60 percent of men adopt nicknames for their workmates compared with only 26 percent of women, who tend to choose more complimentary names. While only 15 percent of men said they had pet names for their loved-ones, 43 percent of women admitted to giving their partners affectionate nicknames.

A racehorse owner who named his horse "Wear the Fox Hat" has been ordered by Jockey Club stewards to call the horse something more appropriate. His second choice, "Hoof Hearted", also was banned.

Why Do We Do That?

Talk radio is the community's compass. It tells us where we've been, where we are now, and where we might be going. Want the background to an issue or the origin of some tradition? The open line will have it. Concerned about what's happening in your world? For solutions ask the expert or press the pollie. Need reassurance about the what lies ahead? Join the switchboard queue for astral predictions. Now, about those origins . . . why do we do that?

Callers can collect quite a few frequent fighter points when they all plunder their reference books for the same required snippet of information at the same time. Inevitably facts are inclined to clash. So we've done a bit of double-checking.

Why Blue for a Boy?

There was a time hundreds of years ago when a male baby was considered his parents' most valuable natural resource. But evil spirits lingered over nurseries poised to snatch any unprotected infant. It was believed the colour blue had the power to combat evil so boys were, where possible, dressed in blue.

Females were of little value. It wasn't until fairly recently that they were associated with the colour pink, and that was thanks mainly to a European folk tale explaining that girl babies were born in pink rosebuds.

Walking Under Ladders

Apart from the obvious safety concerns, people originally avoided ladders because the triangle formed by a ladder leaning against a wall symbolised the Trinity or, in some non-Christian religions, Life. Breaking it was a sign of disrespect so grave it would gratify the Devil.

Tossing Salt over the Shoulder

To the ancient Greeks, salt was sacred and spilling it was unlucky. Even early Christians treated salt with reverence. We're assured by our source that Christ's betrayer, Judas Iscariot, is depicted knocking over the salt in da Vinci's painting 'The Last Supper'.

To blind evil spirits lurking around the left side of your body, toss spilled salt over that shoulder with your 'good' right hand.

Why We Button up on Different Sides

Men started using buttons for fastening clothes in the 13th Century. As the majority were right handed, buttons were stitched onto the side most convenient for doing up while leaving a flap into which the sword hand could be tucked to keep it warm.

It wasn't till the 19th Century that some of the fiddly hooks and lacing on women's garments were replaced with tiny and often expensive buttons. As ladies who could afford such fashionable clothes also employed maids to help them dress, the buttons were on the other side for easier handling.

Driving on the Left

Blame the Brits and the 12th Century Pope Boniface for this one. The Pope decreed that all pilgrims to Rome should keep to the left and the habit persisted in England. Also, free and speedy access to a sword worn traditionally on the left was important for a right-handed horseman to defend himself and his charges.

While Britain's colonial empire stuck with keeping-to-the-left, French revolutionaries asserted their right to reverse the rule. Napoleon, too, scorned enemy influences from across the Channel and insisted for 'strategic' reasons that all his armies should march on the right side.

Easter Eggs

The word 'Easter' is derived from a German spring goddess, Eostre. Her sacred creature was the hare which we now know as the Easter Bunny.

Decorated eggs are a symbol of new life and many European communities included them in their end-of-winter festivals along with spicy 'four seasons' or 'four phases of the moon' bread rolls that used up leftover dried fruit.

Early Christian church leaders adapted the pagan spring customs to fit in with the celebration of Christ's crucifixion and resurrection, re-naming the rolls as hot-cross buns.

Tipping

Tipping as we know it now probably originated in London's flourishing 18th Century coffee houses. These were the meeting places of businessmen, intellectuals and artists who would spend hours socialising and debating. Customers who wanted quick service would place coins in a box marked 'To Insure Promptness', T.I.P.

By chance, years earlier the expression 'Tip' was used by thieves to denote an extra share of booty, or tip of the sack.

X Marks the Spot

Why does 'X' symbolise a kiss? The Vikings unwittingly started the custom. Among the ancient Nordic symbols or runes an 'X' represented a gift or partnership.

Later, in the Middle Ages, both scholars and illiterate people used the 'X' to sign documents. As this was also the symbol of St Andrew, many would then reverently kiss the cross they had just written.

Victorian lovers took the symbol to heart, literally sealing their billet-doux with a kiss, then marking the spot where their lips had touched with an 'X'.

The Origin of 'Jazz'

In the early 1900s cheap brothels in New Orleans provided a loose style of improvised music to pull in the clients. The brothels' Cajun prostitutes were called 'jazz belles', a corruption of 'Jezebels', so the music was eventually referred to as 'jazz'.

Why ℞ for Prescription?

The R is sourced from the Greek word for recipe, 'to take'. Roman apothecaries headed their prescriptions with Rj, the 'j' signifying the god Jupiter: Protector of People. This was reduced to the now familiar ℞.

Why Red for Danger and Dignitaries?

In the Western world the colour red has always symbolised anger, fire, sacrifice, blood and revolution, partly because it was the easiest colour to detect at a distance by day or night.

This century it's been used as the most widely recognised warning signal—on the railway, the beach, the highway, in aircraft, hospitals, space craft and even in radio stations; a flashing red light usually spells trouble.

It was Cleveland Ohio that introduced the first red and green traffic signals in 1914. The amber light was added in New York four years later.

From the 6th century BC, in ancient civilisations red dye was the most difficult and expensive to extract so it symbolised wealth and importance. Hence the red carpet.

St Valentine's Day

The anonymous declaration of love on February 14th has nothing to do with the 3rd Century saint martyred by the Romans. It was the English poet Geoffrey Chaucer who initiated this custom by writing in the late 1300s that birds choose their mates on St Valentine's Day.

Medieval romantic poets enlarged on the theme, and by the 1600s hand decorated love tokens were being delivered to sweethearts. In 1848, American spinster Esther Howland successfully introduced the Valentine card to the USA.

Hallowe'en

The ancient Celtic festival of Samhain, held on November 1st to mark the dying of the year and return of the dead to the mortal world, was also a convenient date on which to slaughter excess farm animals before winter. Samhain fires were lit on every hilltop to fuel the sun through the dark months, and the feast included pagan rituals and games such as trick-or-treat for children.

Instead of banning these riotous goings-on, the early Christian church turned Samhain Day into All Saints, or Hallows, Day. In 1605 political opportunist King James I ordered the lighting of bonfires to be moved to November 5th to celebrate Guy Fawkes' failure to blow up Parliament.

Yours Sincerely

Each time you end a letter with 'Yours sincerely', you're acknowledging an ancient form of quality control. Roman sculptors often concealed cracks in apparently flawless marble statues with melted beeswax. When the wax dried and crumbled, the angry purchaser sought compensation. Reputable sculptors guaranteed their work as *sine sera*, which means *without wax*. Hence 'Yours sincerely'.

The Question Mark?

This hook-shaped character is derived from the first and last letters of the Latin word for question, QUAESTRO. The letters were placed one above the other to save time and space, and this evolved into today's symbol.

Two-fingered Salute

To Sir Winston Churchill it meant 'V for victory'. To hippies it conveyed a message of 'peace, man'. But the first vulgar two-fingered salute goes back to the early 1400s when English and Welsh archers wreaked havoc among French forces at the battles of Agincourt and Crecy.

Following the humiliating defeat, the French swore that any English longbowmen captured would have their first two bowstring-drawing fingers chopped off. Whenever facing the enemy, gesturing with these fingers with palm towards the body became a common English taunt.

Flies in Men's Trousers

Actually the 'fly' was originally the flap that neatly and discreetly covered the buttons or lacing used to fasten the front of sailors' trousers. It's an old British naval term applied to unsecured ropes, flags and sails.

Thumbs Up

This simple gesture has signified approval or encouragement in some northern European countries since the 17th century. It's possibly connected with the earlier custom of sealing an agreement by touching thumbs.

Movies depicting Roman emperors signalling the fate of a gladiator with a thumbs up or down gesture are historically incorrect. It never happened. But it's believed spectators did extend their thumbs from a fist if they wished the gladiator to die, and hid them under curled fingers if he was to be spared.

Alan Jones (2UE)

18 Foot-in-mouth Hall of Fame

No matter how experienced and articulate the man at the mike might be, one slip of the tongue or one second's inattention can propel him into the Foot-in-mouth Hall of Fame. Read what you will into the lack of female presenters in the following line-up. Several were approached for their more toe-curling tales but the response was er, slow, perhaps suggesting—quite logically—that cock-ups are restricted to males. Many thanks to all who answered the call.

Alan Jones—2UE

I wish I could claim I have never been conned. But I can't.

2UE program director John Brennan deserves the credit for this very clever scam. I was coaching the Australian Rugby Seven-a-side Team in Hong Kong in 1985. It was a long weekend, and the Monday was April the first. So I was conducting my regular broadcast from a hotel room.

Down the line from Sydney came the announcement, 'we've got Nana Mouskouri on the line . . .'. Actually, I had interviewed her many times, and I enjoyed her music. On an earlier occasion we had talked about recording a duet for charity if she could gather up sufficient forbearance, so I thought it would be a chat between old acquaintances.

The 'imposter' at the other end of the line was an English professional actress, and she did a phenomenal job. From me it was 'lovely to hear your voice again', and 'let's play some of your beautiful music'. I had been caught hook, line and sinker.

As a broadcaster you can practice as much caution as you like. But if your staff members are devious enough, you could finish up as I did then. I claim it will never happen again. But my staff might differ.

Howard Sattler—6PR

A popular Wednesday morning feature on the weekday 8.30am to noon *Sattler File* is a talkback segment called *Only Human*. It deals with human frailties and foibles, and some of the predicaments in which, too often, we find ourselves. As a measure of its MQ (Minefield Quotient), *Only Human* introduced me to my second wife and led to the end of my first marriage.

My co-host is Despene, also known as Anne Tenna, the breakfast program's television critic and a former section editor of the West Australian newspaper. Our subject on the day in question was 'The First Time'.

Callers were invited to describe the nuts and bolts, so to speak, of how they lost their virginity. Who could have predicted that one of the first to phone in would be Tony, whom I pressed to reveal the details, in all their glory, of how he deflowered . . . our blushing Despene? Oops!

Tony Pilkington—5AA

(half of radio's madcap duo BAZ & PILKO*)*

In 1964 while working at 3YB Warrnambool, I was advised by the then Program Director, David Swinson, that the Funeral Announcements scheduled for 6.40pm were to be treated with the utmost respect. They were costing the local undertaker Jack Guyett the sum of one guinea each, so in no circumstances was the announcer allowed to deviate from the script or ad-lib.

On completing three funeral notices, and not once having made comment on some of the unusual middle names or funeral arrangements, I had two minutes to fill in before the 6.45pm feature—*Hop Harrigan*. It was then that my lack of experience and, dare I say, preparation caught me out. The record I put on was Laurence Welk and his orchestra playing *So Long, It's Been Good to Know You*. I started the next week at 2QN Deniliquin.

Greg Carey—4BC

It was more a motor-mouth situation than foot-in-mouth. I was talking by phone on air with prominent Rugby League Coach Tommy Raudonikis who is a much-loved 'character' of the game.

The interview ran its uneventful course then, several minutes later, a sheepish Tommy rang me back. He had a problem. During our chat he'd taken his false teeth out and put them on top of a nearby car. By the time he remembered, the car had gone!

What followed will go down in airwave annals as The Tracking of Tommy's Teeth. Thanks to countless alert listeners, thirty minutes later a car proudly bearing a set of dentures on its roof was spotted. Coach and choppers were reunited.

Bob Francis—5AA

As regular listeners know, I don't have time for wankers and scumbags on my weekday evening talkback session. But I do enjoy fulfilling the more reasonable requests. As I pioneered talkback in South Australia in 1967, you'd think by now I could spot a screw-up coming. Not so.

It was December, and I was called on the open line by a public-spirited man who had set up a Christmas light display outside his house for others to enjoy. All he needed to complete the show was a friendly Santa Claus, someone with a red suit, a twinkle in his eye and a good line in 'ho, ho, ho' to add to the magic.

I broadcast the request several times and all seemed well. Two months later this big-hearted individual called my program on another matter. I recognised the voice and asked how he had got on with his festive display. Did the Santa I found for him do a good job? 'Oh, yes', he said. 'He was an excellent Father Christmas. Very jolly . . . and he ran off with my wife!'

Neil Mitchell—3AW

It was the first week of the AFL football finals. I was outraged! Outraged because there would be no football game in Melbourne on the Saturday.

My radio editorial thundered out of the 9am news: 'This is the home of football. Don't these people understand you cannot insult Melbourne like this? The interstate teams are taking over! There are games in Perth, Adelaide and Sydney, but the Melbourne supporter stands insulted . . .' and so it went on. I was merciless.

Ending with a savage sting, I cued in the live interview . . . 'On the line, football commentator Rex Hunt.' He seemed oddly hesitant. 'Er, well Neil. It looks like I might be a bit lonely, because I thought I was going to the MCG tomorrow to see . . .'

Yes. I had misread the game fixtures. The major game that weekend was in Melbourne. I was totally, completely, unbelievably wrong. That is a word you rarely hear on talk radio, but I grovelled immediately. Rex tried to help. 'I think, what you probably mean is it's a pity there're not more games in Melbourne.' 'No Rex,' I said. 'I stuffed up.' Apart from that, in 12 years I have done nothing wrong whatsoever.

Jeremy Cordeaux—5DN

The 11.45am weather report on the Cordeaux Show was presented each weekday live and in appropriately serious tones by a Bureau of Meteorology spokesman. On this day, as usual, my assistant producer phoned the duty forecaster and put her name, Louise, up on the studio monitor.

'Louise,' I started. 'It's so nice to have a lady on the line for a change. What's in store for us? What does your seaweed tell you?'

For a Met. Office official her personality was unusually bubbly; even flirty when we explored other uses of seaweed and what else she could see from her window besides cold fronts. What her answers lacked in facts and figures they certainly made up for in entertainment.

The next day at 11.45am I was instructed that Bruce was on the line and ready with the weather.

'Bruce', I said. 'That's two new forecasters in a row. Is the Bureau being expanded?' 'Oh, no,' came the reply. 'Yesterday you spoke to my wife.' And, like Louise, Bruce provided us all with a delightfully casual if unscientific view of the weather.

I wondered over this new human approach to a somewhat dry subject . . . until I learnt the truth. My assistant producer had been calling a wrong number. But, by amazing good fortune, the couple she happened to reach were incredibly helpful people who were determined not to let some strange man on the radio down.

Terry Laidler—3LO

I had just interviewed the 'Chief Frog Keeper' about a colony of frogs being repatriated to Hong Kong airport's man-made island. We then offered a family pass to the zoo and other prizes to the caller with the best or funniest frog call.

People phoned in with the standard 'rivets' and 'knee deeps' plus a few amusing originals, and the 7am news was almost upon us.

TL: Our last caller is Anna from Middle Park. Hello Anna.

Anna: (very small voice): Hello Mr Laidler.

TL: How old are you Anna?

Anna: I'm eight.

TL: (trying to move it along): And what does your frog say, Anna?

Anna: Pobble-bonk, pobble-bonk.

TL: (looking for a quick, witty way out): Very good Anna, but we wanted to know what your frog said, not what it did. We'll announce the winner after the news. It's seven o'clock on 3LO.

During the news the switchboard went berserk. How was I to know that the most endangered species of frog in the whole of Victoria was the Pobble-bonk, so-called because of its distinctive call? Or that every second and third grade kid in the state knew this, having spent that year studying frogs as environmental indicators with a special focus on the Pobble-bonk?

A second family pass to the zoo was quickly arranged.

John Vincent

(one of talk radio's senior statesmen)
As a young, green announcer in the early 1960s I was unaware of the malevolence lurking in the panel of knobs and switches before me. It struck first at 2RE Taree on Anzac Day. All I had to do was put the large black record containing the next pre-recorded program onto the turntable, cue up the needle, make the announcement and get on with my other chores.

It was a special feature to mark the day, a moving mix of war memories and music. My mistake was assuming it would be safe for me to take a leisurely toilet break.

Speakers were located in corridors in the studio area but not in the lavatory, so I failed to hear when the needle got stuck in the record. And what word was it repeating over and over and over again? 'Bloody'.

The second attack occurred at 5KA Adelaide. This time it was Remembrance Day, when all radio stations fall silent for two minutes at the eleventh hour, on the eleventh day of the eleventh month as a mark of respect for our valiant war dead. The trouble was, no-one had alerted the radio station engineer.

As soon as an apparent break in transmission was detected, an emergency tape automatically activated. To my dismay, the song that burst forth over the air shattering the silence was 'Come Back Again . . .' by Daddy Cool.

Richard Glover—2BL

(*author of* Grin and Bear It)
A good part of my years at the *Herald* has been spent sitting safely behind my computer terminal writing television columns; long, carping, ever-so-superior lists of the mistakes made by oh-so-stupid newsreaders and radio program hosts. So, when I was invited to join 2BL as a member of its 'summer relief' team, I had a reputation to protect.

As my greatest fear was mispronunciations, it was inevitable that the topic of the first live-to-air interview set up by my producer was to be a real tongue-tripper; in this case the Romanian dictator Nicolae Ceausescu. 'Ah yes,' I said in my best urbane, know-it-all voice. 'Cheesesquecow, I mean Cowquestkoo, I mean Choosesquuse, oh dammit!' The show started. My panic mounted.

Unbelievably, I then managed to conduct a fifteen minute in-depth interview with ABC European correspondent Lee Duffield in which *not once* did I mention the subject by name. I asked questions about the death of 'the late Romanian president', about the wife of 'the former Romanian dictator' and about the arrest of the son of 'the deposed leader'.

And Finally . . .

The English Advantage

English is not only the mother tongue of over 330 million people, it's also the world's richest language. The Oxford English Dictionary lists some 500,000 English words. By comparison, the Germans cope with a vocabulary of 185,000 words, and the French barely muddle through with fewer than 100,000. Wearing 'pedant' as a badge of honour, intrepid talk radiophiles have taken it upon themselves to protect the English language from the phone-in Philistines, pouncing on every mispronunciation and grammatical goof:

Top Ten Pedants' Pet Hates

- **Et cetera:** pron. **et**-cetera, not ek-cetera;
- **H:** pron. **aitch**, not hhhaitch;
- **Divisive:** pron. dee-**vice**-ive, not dee-viz-iv;
- **Memo:** pron. **mem**-o, not mee-mo. It's from the Latin memorandum;
- **Menu:** pron. **men**-yu, not mee-new;
- **Nuclear:** pron. new-**clee**-ar, not new-kew-lar;
- **Remuneration:** pron. re-**mew**-neration, not re-new-meration;
- **Route:** pron. **root**, not rout, which means something entirely different;
- **Basic:** pron. **base**-ik, not bass *(as in crass)*-ik;
- **Nothing, something, anything:** do *not* end in 'k'.

Also, to set a good example for the next generation of talkback talent (and correct a surprising number of talkshow hosts):

- A picture is hung, a person is **hanged**;
- It's 'none of them **is** . . .', not 'none of them are . . .' (none is short for 'not one');
- '**Maroon**' rhymes with 'balloon', not 'alone';
- There's no 'n' in '**restaurateur**';
- 'Ali was a boxing phenomena' is **wrong.** The singular is **phenomenon.**

And the 'you/I' dilemma continues to present problems.

- 'So, what does this mean to you and **me**?', is correct; 'So, what does this mean to you and **I**?' is wrong.

o, there you have it . . .

the Trash and the Treasure,

the Wit and the Wisdom.

If you are one of the many who contributed, give yourself a pat on the back. This book is yours. Just remember there are six words a talkshow presenter never wants to hear. They are, of course:

'When all is said and done . . .'

which, as long as you're at the other end of the talkback line, it never will be.